Let's Enjoy Science & Tech English

教養課程の科学技術英語

佐藤 哲三 保健医療経営大学特任教授

棈松 伸二 鹿児島工業高等専門学校名誉教授

鞍掛 哲治 鹿児島工業高等専門学校教授

科学技術英語英文提供者

篠田 義明 早稲田大学名誉教授

NAN'UN-DO

Let's Enjoy Science & Tech English

by
Tetsuzo SATO
Shinji ABEMATSU
Tetsuharu KURAKAKE

Download Audio

音声ファイル
無料 DL
のご案内

このテキストの音声を無料で視聴（ストリーミング）・ダウンロードできます。自習用音声としてご活用ください。
以下のサイトにアクセスしてテキスト番号で検索してください。

https://nanun-do.com　テキスト番号［**512062**］

※ 無線 LAN（WiFi）に接続してのご利用を推奨いたします。

※ 音声ダウンロードは Zip ファイルでの提供になります。
お使いの機器によっては別途ソフトウェア（アプリケーション）の導入が必要となります。

Read by
Ryan Drees

※ Let's Enjoy Science & Tech English 音声ダウンロードページは以下の QR コードからもご利用になれます。

はじめに

本書は，科学技術英語に触れつつも基礎英語の復習もできる少し欲張った内容の教材です．このようにせざるを得ない理由があるからです．世の中には数多くの科学技術英語テキストが出ていますが，当然と言えば当然かもしれませんが，そのほとんどが科学技術英語に偏りすぎていて，教養課程レベルで英語の基礎の復習・確認ができるものがないのが実状です．従って，教養課程で科学技術系のテキストを使うのに二の足を踏んでいる先生方が少なからずおられるということをよく耳にします．そこで，教養課程においても使用できる科学技術英語テキストを作成することにしました．

小学校から始めて，中学校を経て高校を卒業して大学や専門学校等に入学するまでに，あるいは中学校を経て高専で三年間学び四年生に進級するまでに，英語を６年以上も学んで来たのに，自信を持って英語を読んだり，書いたり，話したり，聴いたりすることができないと思う人が意外に多いのではないでしょうか．その大きな原因のひとつに英文法力不足を挙げることができるでしょう．

よく言われることですが，母語である日本語環境の中で生まれ育った人が，英語に限らず，一般に外国語をある一定の期間で習得しようと思えば，発音や語彙の学習は勿論のこと，十分な文法学習が必要となります．中学校，高校の６年間の英語学習で，英文法を身に付ける時間は十分確保できているでしょうか．学年が進行するにつれて英語嫌い，英文法嫌いが増えることから，不十分ではないかと思われます．この点を解決しなければこの先も思うように英語力が身につかないでしょう．

本書では，学習事項が１５章に配分され，各章は，第一部 **[Science & Tech English Article]** と第二部 **[Grammar Check]** に分かれます．まず **[Science & Tech English Article]** では，語句注と **Vocabulary** を利用して科学技術英文の精読をして，**Q & A** でまとめます．次に **[Grammar Check]** では，上記のことと TOEIC や実用英語技能検定等の各種英検に配慮して，英語の基礎固めと確認ができるように，「英文法」のまとめと練習問題をこなした後，「並べ替え」，「英作」が続き，各章の文法項目に囚われない「書き換え」が加えられています．そして最後に **Road to Science & Tech English** で様々な科学技術英文を正確・明快かつ無駄なく表現する術を学ぶことにします．このように本書を通して，科学技術英語に親しみながら基本英語の学習もしっかりできます．

最後に，本書の出版を快諾された南雲堂の南雲一範社長，編集実務の行き届いたご配慮をいただいた加藤敦氏に心より感謝申し上げます．

2020 年　秋
著者一同

CONTENTS

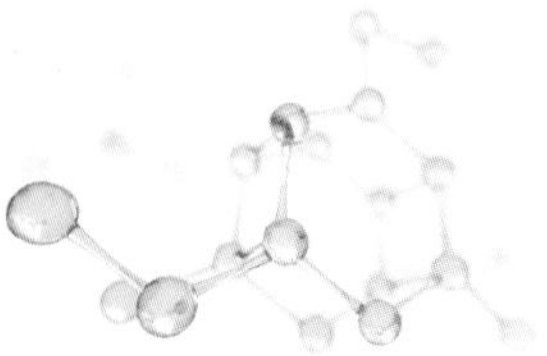

Construction of Atoms

（原子の構造）

2

Just as there is always a powerful attraction between two *unlike* electric charges, so there is a powerful repulsive force between two *like* electric charges. Two electrons brought closely together will fly apart. Two protons brought together will also fly apart—if neutrons are not present to hold them together. The neutrons supply a sort of binding force, or nuclear "glue," to hold the two protons together in the nucleus of the helium atom.

A neutron has approximately the same weight as a proton. Thus, with 2 neutrons and 2 protons, the helium atom weighs four times as much as a hydrogen atom. On this account helium is said to have an atomic weight of 4. The weight of the electrons is neglected in this calculation, since it takes 1,840 electrons to weigh as much as one proton or one neutron.

If, instead of 2 protons, the nucleus of an atom should contain 3 protons, we would normally find 4 neutrons in that nucleus. This combination gives us, instead of a gas, a solid—the metal lithium. Three electrons normally circle the lithium nucleus. The lithium atom, with 3 protons and 4 neutrons, has an atomic weight of 7.

From these facts it should be clear that to change the number of protons and neutrons in an atom is to change the atom from one element into another element.

Words & Phrases: **just as A, as B** ちょうどＡのようにＢ　**attraction**（物質間の）引力 cf. gravity（地球・宇宙の引力），affinity（元素間の引力）　***unlike*** = different, dissimilar　**electric charges** 電荷：物質が正か負に電気を帯びること　**repulsive force** 斥力 opp. attraction　**electrons** 電子：負電荷で原子の構成要素　**(which are) brought**（ ）内は挿入句　**bring A together** Ａを結び付ける　**will fly apart** 跳び離れる wii は現在の習性　**protons** 陽子：正電荷で原子核の構成要素　**neutron** 中性子：原子核の構成要素 cf. neuter：ラテン語で neither（両方ともない）のこと　**hold A together** Ａを結び付ける　**a sort of A** 一種の**Ａ**　**binding force, or nuclear "glue"** 結合力，つまり核の膠（にかわ）　**nucleus** = atomic nucleus 原子核，核と略称　**the same A as B** Ｂと同じＡ　**four times as much as A** Ａの４倍の　**hydrogen atom** 水素原子　**on this account** こういう理由で　**atomic weight** 原子量：質量数 12 の炭素の同位体の原子量を 12 とし，これを基準に他の元素について定めた原子の質量　**instead of** …の代わりに　**combination** 結合：２つ以上の物質が反応して結合し，全く別の１物質となる化学変化　**metal lithium** リチウム金属：固体の単体中最も軽い　**element** 元素：物質を化学的に分けて行き最後に得られる要素

Vocabulary

語頭文字と文字数をヒントに綴りなさい．

01. 構造 c-(12字)	02. 原子 a-(4)	03. 強力な p-(8)	04. 同様な l-(4)
05. 電子 e-(8)	06. 接近して c-(7)	07. 存在して p-(7)	08. 供給する s-(6)
09. 核の n-(7)	10. にかわ g-(4)	11. ヘリウム h-(6)	12. 大体 a-(13)
13. 重さ w-(6)	14. 従って t-(4)	15. 重さが～ある w-(5)	16. 無視する n-(7)
17. 計算 c-(11)	18. 入っている c-(7)	19. 固体 s-(5)	20. 周りを回る c-(6)
21. 事実 f-(4)	22. のはずだ s-(6)	23. 明らかな c-(5)	24. 数 n-(6)

Q & A

1) What is there between two different electric charges?

2) How will two electrons move if they are brought closely together?

3) How much more does the helium atom weigh than a hydrogen atom?

4) How many electrons does it take to weigh as much as one proton or one neutron?

5) What moves all the way around the lithium nucleus?

Chapter 1-2 [Grammar Check]　5つの基本文型

1. 第1文型 …主語 (S) + 完全自動詞 (V)

1) **Birds sing.**
2) The **sun sets** in the west.
3) Several **boys are running** around the lake every morning.
4) **Julia chatted** with her friend over coffee.
5) There **is** a **dog** at the door.

---

2. 第2文型 …主語 (S) + 不完全自動詞 (V) + 主格補語 (SC)

6) **He is** a **surgeon**.
7) **She is busy** every day.
8) **Alice looks happy**.
9) **She feels better** than this morning.
10) The **leaves** have **turned red** in the mountains.

---

3. 第3文型 …主語 (S) + 完全他動詞 (V) + 目的語 (O)

11) **I like dogs.**
12) **They play football** every day.
13) **They enjoyed riding horses**.
14) **Rachel** often **loses** her **key**.
15) **They stopped talking** when the teacher came in.

---

4. 第4文型 …主語 (S) + 完全他動詞 (V) + 間接目的語 (IO) + 直接目的語 (DO)

16) My **uncle gave me** a **camera**. = My uncle gave a camera **to** me.
17) **I wrote him** a long **letter**. = I wrote a long letter **to** him.
18) **He bought me** this **bike**. = He bought this bike **for** me.
19) **She cooked him meals**. = She cooked meals **for** him.
20) **They asked her** some **questions**. = They asked some questions **of** her.

---

4. 第5文型 …主語 (S) + 不完全他動詞 (V) + 目的語 (O) + 目的格補語 (OC)

21) **We call him Ken**.
22) **He named** his **son Taro**.
23) **They made her happy**.
24) **I found** this **book** very **interesting**.

Exercises

A. 次の英文の文型を述べなさい.

1. He was a student at this school.
2. I will stay with my aunt.
3. Keep your eyes closed.
4. I made Shun a new doghouse.
5. I quite forgot her birthday.

B. 次の英文の下線部が目的語か補語かを答えなさい.

1. Rachel is playing the piano.
2. She will be a star player in the future.
3. His brother got angry over trifles.
4. My uncle told me an interesting story.
5. They made me happy.

C. 次の英文の下線部の語句を文末に移動させなさい.

1. Ben offered Alice his help.
2. They asked me several questions.
3. I'll soon get you a pillow.
4. Jack will buy Jill a beautiful comb.
5. Please lend me ten dollars.

D. 次の英文を日本文に直しなさい.

1. The football season has already begun.
2. Seeing is believing.
3. You must write a letter in English.
4. I found the book very interesting.
5. She made me a Christmas cake.

E. 次の各組の文が同じ意味になるように, (　) 内に適語を書き入れなさい.

1. He is a hard worker. = He (　　　　　) (　　　　　).
2. They lived happily. = They lived a (　　　　　) (　　　　　).
3. Why did you say so? = (　　　　　) made you say so?
4. This bike belongs to me. = This bike is (　　　　　).
5. She can speak English well. = She is a (　　　　　) (　　　　　) of English.

Rearranging ▶▶▶ [ ] 内の語に語頭文字が示された語を加えて並べ替え，和文に合う英文にしなさい.

1. それらの部屋はどれも南向きではない. [(f) / of / the / neither / south / rooms].

2. 法の下では全ての人間は平等である.
[(a) / humans / the / law / all / equal / under].

3. 彼はその次の日に日本から中国に向かった.
[(l) / Japan / the / he / for / next / China / day].

4. 冷蔵庫は魚や肉を新鮮に保ってくれる.
[(k) / fish / the / and / fresh / refrigerator / meat].

5. 父はよく私たちに興味深い話をしてくれた.
[(t) / often / to / my / stories / father / us / interesting].

Basic Composition ▶▶▶ 文末の（ ）内の条件をヒント（動詞は原形で提示）に英訳しなさい.

1. 昨夜 , Tom は Jane と踊った. (6 語で)

2. 空には雲ひとつなかった. (8 語で)

3. その結果はがっかりさせるようなものであった. (4 語で)

4. 彼女の兄さんは年の割には若く見える. (for を使い 7 語で)

5. 君は彼が私たちに言いたかったことがわかりましたか. (what, tell を使い 9 語で)

6. 一昨日，私は岩手にいる伯父に手紙を書いた. (13 語で)

7. コンピューターは私たちの手間を大いに省いてくれる. (save, work を使い 8 語で)

8. 彼が私に魚の釣り方を教えてくれた. (show, how を使い 7 語で)

9. その知らせを聞いて彼らは喜んだ. (make を使い 5 語で)

10. 彼女は車をよく整備して (in good condition) いる. (7 語で)

Rewriting ▶▶▶ 次の各組の文がほぼ同じ意味になるように，（　）内に適語を書き入れなさい．

1. I won't lend anyone my bicycle. = I won't lend my bicycle (　　　　　) anyone.
2. You are allowed to take a picture here. = You (　　　　　) take a picture here.
3. He must have taken the wrong train. = It is certain that he (　　　　　) the wrong train.
4. She is two years older than I am. = She is older than I am (　　　　　) two years.
5. However tired he is, he gets up at five.
   = No matter (　　　　　) tired he is, he gets up at five.
6. Five years have passed since they got married.
   = They have (　　　　　) married for five years.
7. You are very kind to do so. = It is very kind (　　　　　) you to do so.
8. As he didn't know what to say, he kept silent.
   = (　　　　　) knowing what to say, he kept silent.
9. This is a picture that he painted himself. = This is a picture of his own (　　　　　).
10. The higher we go up, the colder the air gets.
   = (　　　　　) we go up higher, the air gets colder.

▶▶▶ Road to Science & Tech English (A1) ▶▶▶

Put into English ▶▶▶ 語句を並べ替えて，日本文に合う英文にしなさい．

1. （ねじなどの）転造工具の交換は非常に簡単で，数分以内でできます．
   (easily and / our rolling tools / within a few minutes / can be replaced).

   ....

2. 台風 10 号により私たちの校舎の窓がすべて吹き飛ばされた．
   (blew out / all the windows / typhoon No. 10 / in the school buildings).

   ....

3. 2 枚の板が重なるところに釘を打ちなさい．
   (two boards / a nail / drive / join / where).

   ....

4. 水の表面はその上の世界を映す大きな鏡である．
   (the world / is / reflecting / above / the water surface / a giant mirror).

   ....

5. 当社は高速で走る車を製造した．
   (high-speed / we / automobiles / manufactured).

   ....

Mechanical Energy
（機械エネルギー）

4

Suppose a heavy steel girder is hoisted high up on a bridge tower. It is lifted, lightly and easily by mechanical energy in the strong steel cables.

Far below on the ground, a powerful diesel engine puts mechanical energy into the cables. A diesel engine converts heat into mechanical energy since it is a heat engine.

Most of the work in this world—hoisting, heaving, pushing, pulling, rolling, drilling, cutting, stamping—is done by the output of mechanical energy. Much of this energy is converted from heat energy.

Mechanical energy has something to do with the way molecules move. When the molecules of an object move together, as a group, the result is mechanical energy. Whatever the state of the molecules may be, they move as a group.

The saw moves as a solid saw against the wood, cutting the wood with mechanical energy. A hammer drives against a nail with mechanical energy. The molecules do not have to be in a solid state to produce mechanical energy. A stream of water molecules flowing against a wheel can make it turn. A flow of gas molecules moving together can push with mechanical energy, turning a windmill or pushing a sailboat.

Mechanical energy is measured in units called foot-pounds.

Words & Phrases: **mechanical energy** 機械エネルギー：力学的な量によって定まるエネルギー **suppose A (that 節)** Aと仮定してみよう **girder** 桁（けた：垂木を受ける横架材）；梁（はり：垂木が掛からず，桁に直行する部材）．beamとも言う． **is hoisted** 高い場所に引き上げられる **high up on a bridge tower** 橋の鉄塔の上高く **lightly** 軽く **steel cables** 鋼線 **Far below on the ground** はるか下の地上では cf. high up on a bridge tower **a powerful diesel engine** 強力なディーゼル・エンジン **puts A into the cables** Aをケーブルに伝達している **converts heat into mechanical energy** 熱エネルギーを機械エネルギーに変える **a heat engine** 熱機関：熱エネルギーを消費して動力を発生する原動機 **hoisting** 巻揚げ（すること） **heaving** 持ち上げ（すること） **rolling** ころがすこと **drilling** 掘削（すること） **stamping** 粉砕すること；型押し **by the output of A** Aの生産（力）により **much of A** Aの大部分 **has (something) to do with A** Aに関係がある **molecule** 分子 **a solid saw** 固体ののこぎり **cutting** = and cut **drives against A** Aに対して打ち下ろされる **in a solid state** 固体状態で **stream** 流れ **flowing** = which flow moving = which move **turning A or pushing B** = and turns A or pushes B **windmill** 風車 **measure** 測定する **unit** 単位 **foot-pounds** フートポンド：1ポンドの重さの物を1フィート揚げる仕事量

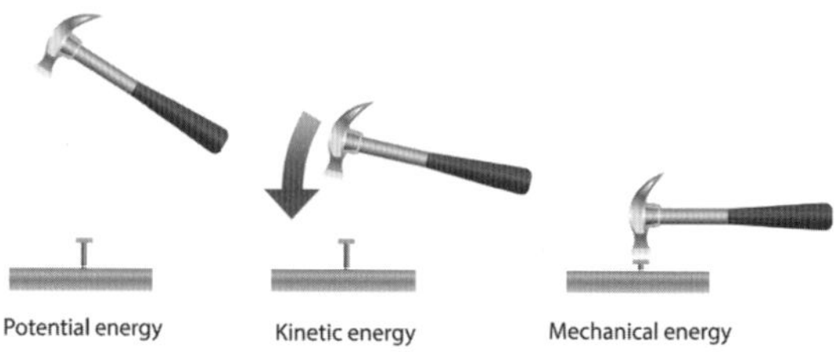

Vocabulary

語頭文字と文字数をヒントに綴りなさい．

01. けた g-(6字)	02. 引き揚げる h-(5)	03. 軽々と l-(7)	04. 鋼線 c-(5)
05. 強力な p-(8)	06. 変わる c-(7)	07. 巻き揚げる h-(5)	08. 持ち上げる h-(5)
09. 転がす r-(4)	10. 粉砕する s-(5)	11. 穴を開ける d-(5)	12. 生産 o-(6)
13. 分子 m-(8)	14. 物質 o-(6)	15. 結果 r-(6)	16. 状態 s-(5)
17. 固体（の） s-(5)	18. 生み出す p-(7)	19. 流れ s-(6)	20. 打ち込む d-(5)
21. 流れ（る） f-(4)	22. 風車 w-(8)	23. 測定する m-(7)	24. 単位 u-(4)

Q & A

1) What is a heavy steel girder lifted lightly and easily by?

2) Why does a diesel engine change heat into mechanical energy?

3) What is mechanical energy concerned with?

4) What makes a hammer drive against nail?

5) How is mechanical energy measured?

Chapter 2-2 [Grammar Check]　動詞

1. be 動詞

5

1) I **am** a medical clerk and he is a pharmacist.
2) I'**m not** busy now. He **isn't** busy, either.
3) How **are** you? I'**m** fine, thank you.
4) Where **were** you yesterday? I **was** in Fukuoka.
5) There **aren't** any children in the park.

---

2. 一般動詞（現在形）

6) I **don't like** dogs.
7) The earth **revolves** around the sun.
8) He **doesn't** usually **have** coffee at meals.
9) **Do** you **know** him very well? No, I **don't**.
10) **Does** Bob **belong** to the baseball club? No, he **doesn't**.
11) Who **cooks** breakfast every morning? Mother **does**. / I **do**.

※ 状態動詞 … be, know, belong, like など
※ 動作動詞 … jump, cross, put, run など

---

3. 一般動詞（過去形）

12) I **slept** well last night.
13) Ben **changed** his dirty clothes for clean ones.
14) I **studied** Latin at school, but I never **did learn** it.　「…全然身につかなかった」
15) Tom **didn't leave** for London yesterday.
16) **Did** the volcano Mt. Sakurajima **erupt** a few days ago? No, it **didn't**.

---

4. 自動詞・他動詞と群動詞

17) The library **opens** at nine.
18) Please **open** the door.
19) Ken is **lying** on his stomach.
20) She **laid** her baby on the bed.
21) When the curtain **rises**, everybody **raises** his or her head.
22) What time will he **arrive in** Tokyo? = What time will he **reach** Tokyo?
23) They **approached** the room without a sound.
24) We **discussed** the matter with the teacher.
25) This fruit **resembles** that one in shape, but not in taste.
26) He didn't **respect** you. = He didn't **look up to** you.
27) She **endured** a week of hard training. = She **put up with** a week of hard training.

Exercises

A. 次の英文の（　）内から適語を選びなさい.

1. There (is, are, was, were) a lot of children here a few hours ago.
2. My father (isn't, don't, doesn't, hasn't) drive on Sundays.
3. When did the plane (take, takes, took, taking) off?
4. She (belongs, is belonging, has belonged) to the tennis club for two years.

B. 次の各組の文が同じ意味になるように（　）内に適語を入れなさい.

1. How many seasons are there in a year? = How many seasons (　　　　　) a year (　　　　　)?
2. Jack is a fast swimmer. = Jack can (　　　　　) (　　　　　).
3. Sachiko is a good speaker of English. = Sachiko (　　　　　) English (　　　　　).
4. We (　　　　　) a lot of snow here in winter. = It (　　　　　) a lot here in winter.

C. 次の日本文を，（　）内の語句に１語を加えて，英文に直しなさい.

1. あの歌の出だしはどうでしたか.（ begin / song / how / that)?
2. 電車はあとどのくらいで博多駅に着きますか.
   (due to / soon / the train / at / how / arrive / Hakata Station)?
3. その小包はどれくらいの重さですか.
   (the parcel / much / weigh / how)? = (heavy / the parcel / how)?
4. 日本ではふつう家に入る前に靴を脱ぎます.
   People (before / usually / their / their / homes / entering / shoes / off) in Japan.

D. 次の各文の（　）内から適当なものを選びなさい.

1. The lawyer insists (in / of / on) the man's innocence.
2. Don't (enter / enter at / enter in) the room without knocking.
3. When did he (marry / marry to / marry with) her?
4. Smoke (rised / rose / raised) from the factory chimneys.
5. They won't agree (about / over / with) me on this point.
6. TOEFL stands (at / for / in) Test of English as a Foreign Language.
7. He consented (of / on / to) my plan.
8. I (attended / attended at / attended to) a funeral last Friday.
9. Who will look (after / at / for) your pet dog while you are on a trip?
10. I'll catch up (on / to / with) you soon.

Rearranging

▶▶▶ [　] 内の語に語頭文字が示された語を加えて並べ替え，和文に合う英文にしなさい．

1. 彼はクラスの他の学生に遅れないように努めている．
[(k　) / up / the other / the class / in / with / to / he / students / tries].

2. 私はバスが遅れるだろうと思っている．
[(e　) / to / late / I / bus / be / the].

3. 人は皆平等に創られている．
[(a　) / men / equal / all / created].

4. トムは友人を訪ねたが，家には誰もいなかった．
[(c　) / his friend, / Tom / home / was / at / on / there / but / nobody].

5. 彼女の行動はいつもながらのいろいろのうわさを生んだ．
[(b　) / rumors / forth / crop of / the usual / her action].

Basic Composition

▶▶▶ 文末の（　）内の条件をヒント（動詞は原形で提示）に英訳しなさい．

1. 私はそのコートを安かったので買った．　(because, cheap を使い 8 語で)

2. 私は 6 時の電車に間に合うように早く起きた．　(the 6:00 train を使い 9 語で)

3. 春にはたくさんの美しい花々が咲く．　(bloom を使い 6 語で)

4. はさみは下から 2 番目の引き出しの中にあります．　(drawer を使い 10 語で)

5. なぜ君は昨日学校に遅れたのですか．　(late を使い 7 語で)

6. 彼女が戻ってくるまでここで待ちましょう．　(until を使い 7 語で)

7. 君が手を貸してくれたのでとても手間が省けました．　(save, lot を使い 8 語で)

8. その提案に賛成ですか，それとも反対ですか．　(for, proposal を使い 7 語で)

9. 誕生日に何が欲しいですか．　(for を使い 7 語で)

10. 明日雨が降れば，私は家にいます．　(stay at を使い 9 語で)

Rewriting ▶▶▶ 次の各組の文がほぼ同じ意味になるように，（ ）内に適語を書き入れなさい．

1. I didn't come in till they were seated.
   = When I came in, they ( ) already been seated.
2. You were not made fun of by anybody. = ( ) made fun of you.
3. She was a nurse of his acquaintance.
   = She was a nurse with whom he was ( ).
4. He denied that he was guilty. = He denied ( ) guilty.
5. Write your name on anything that you have.
   = Write your name on ( ) you have.
6. It is time for you to go to bed. = It is time you ( ) to bed.
7. Why does the baby cry like that? = ( ) makes the baby cry like that?
8. I wish we had no examinations. = If ( ) we had no examinations.
9. I cannot help feeling sorry for her. = I cannot ( ) feel sorry for her.
10. He made a quick decision. = He ( ) quickly.

▶▶▶ Road to Science & Tech English (A2) ▶▶▶

Put into English ▶▶▶ 語句を並べ替えて，日本文に合う英文にしなさい．

1. その室に取り付けられている大抵の装置はその場にはふさわしくない．
   (for the occasion / installed / are not suitable / in the chamber / most devices).

   ....

2. はんだ付けをする線はきれいに研がねばならない．
   (of the wires / will be soldered / clean / together / the surface / that).

   ....

3. これらの新型機は旧式のものと急速に入れ替わっている．
   (are rapidly / ones / these / the older / new machines / replacing).

   ....

4. ブラケット A の位置調整は工場でもしてありますので，いじらないでください．
   (and it / is / must be left alone / the Bracket A position / a factory-determined adjustment).

   ....

5. 本論文では，連続的に，かつ，ゆっくりと負荷が加えられている金属棒の挙動を論じている．
   The behavior (is discussed / applied load / a metal bar / a continuously and slowly / of / under / in this paper).

   ....

Friction
(摩擦)

6

Friction is the resistance that one surface offers to the movement over another surface. The amount of friction depends upon the nature of the two surfaces, and the forces which hold them together.

In many instances friction is useful. The cinders you throw under the wheels of your car when it is slipping on an icy pavement increase the friction. You wear rubber-soled shoes to keep from slipping. And locomotives carry a lot of sand which can be dropped on the tracks in front of the driving wheels to increase the friction between the wheels and the track. Nails hold structures together because of the friction between the nails and the lumber.

When you are trying to stop an object in motion, you make friction work. But when you want a machine to run smoothly and at high efficiency, you eliminate as much friction as possible by oiling and greasing bearings, and honing and smoothing rubbing surfaces.

Whenever you apply force to cause motion, friction makes the actual mechanical advantage fall short of the theoretical mechanical advantage. Because of friction, you have to make a greater effort to overcome the resistance which you want to remove. If you place a marble and a lump of sugar on a table and give each an equal push, the marble will move farther. This is because rolling friction is always less than sliding friction. You take advantage of this fact whenever you use ball bearings or roller bearings. Remember that rolling friction is always less than sliding friction.

Words & Phrases: **friction** （2つの物体の）摩擦　**resistance** 抵抗　**offers to the movement over ~** ～上の運動に与える　**in many instances** 多くの場合　**cinders** 炭がら　**icy pavement** 氷の張った舗装道路　**pavement** ［英］歩道．米で歩道は sidewalk　**keep from slipping** 滑らないようにする　**locomotives** 機関車　**tracks** 鉄道線路 = lines of metal rails for cars to go on　**driving wheels** 駆動輪　**hold ~ together** ～をしっかりと留める　**because of ~** ～のために　**an object in motion** 運動中の物体　**you make friction work** 君は摩擦を働かせる　**run** = operate　**at high efficiency** 効率よく　**eliminate** 取り除く　**as much ~ as possible** できる限り多くの～　**by oiling and greasing bearings** ベアリング（軸受）に油をさしたりグリースを塗ることにより　**honing** とぎ上げる　**rubbing surfaces** 摩擦面　**apply force to cause motion** 力を使って動かす　**friction makes the actual mechanical advantage fall short of the theoretical mechanical advantage** 摩擦の為に，実際上の力学的利点が理論上の力学的利点に達しなくなる　**make a greater effort** より多くの努力をする　**rolling friction** ころがり摩擦　**sliding friction** すべり摩擦　**take advantage of ~** ～を利用する　**ball bearings** ボール・ベアリング，玉軸受　**roller bearings** ローラー・ベアリング，ころ軸受

Vocabulary

語頭文字と文字数をヒントに綴りなさい．

01.	抵抗	r-(10字)	02.	摩擦	f-(8)	03.	量	a-(6)	04.	力	f-(5)
05.	炭がら	c-(6)	06.	舗装道路	p-(8)	07.	ゴム	r-(6)	08.	機関車	l-(10)
09.	鉄道線路	t-(5)	10.	くぎ	n-(4)	11.	つかむ	h-(4)	12.	構造物	s-(9)
13.	材木	l-(6)	14.	滑らかに	s-(8)	15.	効率	e-(10)	16.	排除する	e-(9)
17.	軸受	b-(7)	18.	磨く	h-(4)	19.	表面	s-(7)	20.	理論上の	t-(11)
21.	打ち勝つ	o-(8)	22.	取り除く	r-(6)	23.	ビー玉	m-(6)	24.	好都合	a-(9)

Q & A

1) What is friction?

2) What should you do when your car is slipping on an icy pavement?

3) Why do nails hold structures together?

4) What do you do when you want a machine to run smoothly and at high efficiency?

5) If you place a marble and a lump of sugar on a table and give each an equal push, which will move farther, a marble or a lump of sugar?

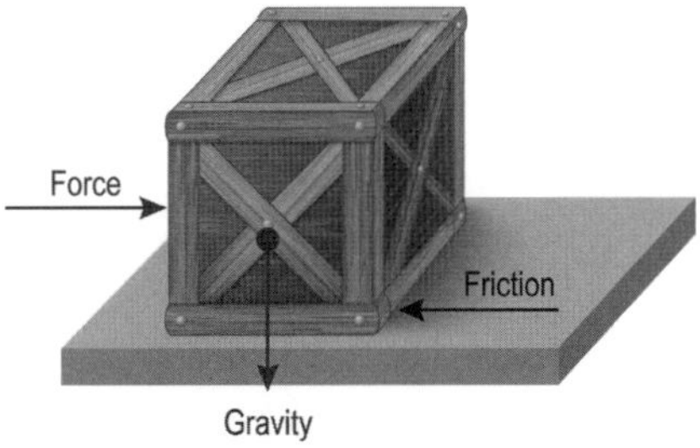

Chapter 3-2 [Grammar Check]　進行形・未来形・助動詞

1. 現在・過去進行形 … 〈be 動詞＋現在分詞〉

7

1) He **is playing** tennis with her.
2) They **are not studying** but **watching** TV.
3) I **was washing** my car then.
4) **Are** you **working** now? — Yes, I **am**.

※ know や belong 等の状態動詞は，原則として進行形にしない.

---

2. 未来形 … 単純未来，意志未来

5) I **will/shall be** twenty years old next month.
6) It **will rain** this afternoon.
7) She **will visit** us next month.
8) I **am going to sell** this car.

---

3. can, must, may, will, shall, should, need, dare, ought to

9) She **can** make sandwiches.
10) **Can** I use your bike?
11) **Can** the news be true?
12) The news **cannot** be true.
13) You **must** study harder than before.
14) He **must** be our teacher.
15) **May** I come in? — Yes, you may. / Yes, please.
16) It **may** snow tonight.
17) **May** you live long!
18) **Will** you open the window? — All right.
19) **Shall I** turn on the radio? — Yes, please.
20) **Shall we** go to the movies? — Yes, let's.
21) You **should** come earlier.
22) You **shouldn't** go out so late at night.
23) You **need not** buy that book.
24) **Need** I go now?
25) I **dared not** tell her the sad news. 「～するだけの勇気がなかった」
26) **How dare** you say such a thing? 「よくもまあ～できるものだ」
27) You **oughtn't to** say such a thing.
28) That **ought to** be an exciting game.

Exercises

A. 次の英文の（　）内から適語を選びなさい.

1. He (used to, should) go to school before by bus, but now by subway.
2. You (mustn't, needn't) make your bed. I will do it.
3. There (would, used to) be a clean stream here.
4. You (ought, should) not to eat so much.
5. (Would, Should) you mind lending me some money?

B. 次の各組の文が同じ意味になるように（　）内に適語を入れなさい.

1. Don't throw a stone at the dog. = You (　　　　　　) throw a stone at the dog.
2. Dick wasn't able to go on a picnic yesterday.
   = Dick (　　　　　　) go on a picnic yesterday.
3. It is not necessary for you to pay the money.
   = You (　　　　　　) pay the money.
4. It is impossible for me to write the report in a day.
   = I (　　　　　　) write the report in a day.
5. Surely she missed the 8:20 train.
   = She (　　　　　　) have missed the 8:20 train.

C. 次の英文を日本文に直しなさい.

1. I will do my best to the last.

   ……………………………………………………………

2. The sun is about to sink below the horizon.

   ……………………………………………………………

3. Can the rumor be true? — No, it can't be.

   ……………………………………………………………

D. 次の日本文を英文に直しなさい.

1. 私が London に着いたとき，雨が降っていました.

   ……………………………………………………………

2. Andrew は間違えてばかりいる.（always を用いて進行形で）

   ……………………………………………………………

3. 私は自動車を売ることにしています.（be going to を用いて）

   ……………………………………………………………

4. 今夜天気はどうなりますか.（What と How を用いて 2 通りで）

   ……………………………………………………………

5. 宿題を手伝ってもらえませんか.

   ……………………………………………………………

Rearranging ▶▶▶ [　] 内の語に語頭文字が示された語を加えて並べ替え，和文に合う英文にしなさい.

1. 私たちは軽井沢で楽しんでいます.
[(h　) / a / at / we / Karuizawa / time / good / are].

2. 隣の犬はいつも吠えてばかりいる.
[(b　) / all / dog / the / my / is / neighbor's / time].

3. 彼女が電話をかけてきたとき , 私は入浴中でした.
[(t　) / called / I / me / she / when / a / was / bath].

4. 彼女はいつも他人のあら捜しばかりしていた.
[(f　) / always / others / fault / was / with / she].

5. 明朝は雪が降っているでしょう.
[(b　) / will / morning / it / snowing / tomorrow].

Basic Composition ▶▶▶ 文末の（　）内の条件をヒント（動詞は原形で提示）に英訳しなさい.

1. トムは先週からずっとジェーンに会えずにいます. (able, see を使い 11 語で)

2. 彼の身に何か起こったのかもしれません. (happen を使い 6 語で)

3. あなた方お二人の幸せを祈ります. (may を使い 5 語で)

4. 君は次の日曜日には出社しなければならないでしょう. (9 語で)

5. 昨夜は激しく雨が降ったに違いない. (7 語で)

6. 私は子供のころよくその湖に釣りに行ったものだ. (would を使い 11 語で)

7. 君はその映画を見ればよかったのに. (should を使い 6 語で)

8. 彼が怒るのは当然です. (natural, should を使い 8 語で)

9. 兄は正午までにはここに着くはずです. (ought を使い 8 語で)

Rewriting ▶▶▶ 次の各組の文がほぼ同じ意味になるように，（　）内に適語を書き入れなさい．

1. He intended to have gone there. = He intended to go there, but he (　　　　　　).
2. We cannot account for tastes. = There is (　　　　　　) accounting for tastes.
3. I said to him, "Where do you live?" = I asked him where he (　　　　　　).
4. Tom was absent from the meeting.
   = Tom absented (　　　　　　) from the meeting.
5. I believe that her remark was true.
   = I believe in the (　　　　　　) of her remark.
6. Recently children have decreased in number.
   = Recently the (　　　　　　) of children has decreased.
7. This is the house in which the writer lived.
   = This is the house (　　　　　　) the writer lived.
8. Certainly, he is guilty. = It is (　　　　　　) that he is guilty.
9. This problem is more than I can understand. = This problem is (　　　　　　) me.
10. He is a fluent speaker of English. = He speaks English (　　　　　　).

▶▶▶ Road to Science & Tech English (A3) ▶▶▶

Put into English ▶▶▶ 語句を並べ替えて，日本文に合う英文にしなさい．

1. その技術者は抵抗器を損傷したシャーシーから取り外した．
   (a resister / the engineer / the damaged chassis / from / removed).

2. 工場で液体をどのように処理するかについての研究が，本論文の目的である．
   The (is discussed / in / in / this paper / our factory / liquid disposal).

3. 使用した材料と実験方法は序文で述べる．
   (used in / are discussed / and methods / in Preface / this experiment / the materials).

4. このようにして製造したケーブルは 150 度を超えない温度で完全かつ十分に乾燥させること．
   (thus manufactured / not higher than 150℃ / and thorough / requires careful / the cable / drying at a temperature).

Temperature and Molecules
（温度と分子）

All forms of matter are made up of very small particles called molecules. These are combinations of atoms (for example, a molecule of water consists of two atoms of hydrogen chemically linked to one atom of oxygen) and the atoms themselves are constructed from even smaller particles—electrons, protons, and neutrons. The molecule, however, is the smallest particle of any substance capable of separate existence. A 'solid object' is in fact an arrangement of a very large number of individual molecules, held in place by inter-molecular forces of attraction and able to resist deformation because of these forces. In thinking of matter in molecular terms and in drawing diagrams to represent its structure, there is a strong tendency to regard the molecules as stationary: but while this is often convenient it does not represent the true state of affairs. An object may be 'at rest' but its molecules are in continuous motion, and this motion is responsible for the effects which we associate with 'temperature,' and for the energy transfer which we call 'heat.' The difference between a hot bar of metal and a cold bar of the same metal is that the molecules of the hot bar are moving faster than those of the cold bar. If the two bars are brought into contact, fast-moving molecules in the hot bar will collide with slower-moving molecules in the cold bar and transfer to them some of their kinetic energy. Thus 'heat' will be transferred until the molecules of both bars are moving at the same speed—that is, until the bars are 'at the same temperature.'

Words & Phrases: **molecules** 分子　**particles** 粒子　**combinations** 結合 cf. chemical combination 化合　**hydrogen** 水素　**chemically linked to ~** 化学的に～と組み合わされた　**electrons** 電子　**protons** 陽子　**neutrons** 中性子　**(which is) capable of separate existence** （個々に）分離して存在できる　**solid object** 固体　**in fact** 事実上　**an arrangement of ~** ～の配列　**held in place** 適所に置かれている　**by inter-molecular forces of attraction** 分子間の引力によって　**resist deformation** 変形に耐える　**In thinking ~ and in drawing ~.** = When we think ~ and when we draw ~.　**in molecular terms** 分子の関係で　**regard A as B** A を B とみなす　**while** = though　**the true state of affairs** 物の実態　**at rest** 静止の　**is responsible for ~** ～のためである　**the effects which we associate with 'temperature'** われわれが温度と連想する影響　**the energy transfer** エネルギー移動　**are brought into contact** 接触するようになる　**collide with ~** ～と衝突する　**transfer to them some of their kinetic energy** = transfer some of their kinetic energy to them 運動エネルギーの幾分かをそれらへ移す ＊目的語句が長くなったので文尾に回ったもの.　**kinetic energy** = motive energy

Vocabulary

語頭文字と文字数をヒントに綴りなさい．(pl. → plural 複数形)

01. 温度 t-(11字)	02. 粒子 p-(8)	03. 結合 c-(11)	04. 水素 h-(8)
05. 酸素 o-(6)	06. 構成する c-(9)	07. 物質 s-(9)	08. 存在 e-(9)
09. 配列 a-(11)	10. 個々の i-(10)	11. 変形 d-(11)	12. 関係 (pl. で) t-(5)
13. 描く d-(4)	14. 図表 d-(7)	15. 表す r-(9)	16. 傾向 t-(8)
17. 静止した s-(10)	18. 便利な c-(10)	19. 物，事 a-(6)	20. 連続的な c-(10)
21. 連想する a-(9)	22. 接触 c-(7)	23. 衝突する c-(7)	24. 移す t-(8)

Q & A

1) What are combinations of atoms?

2) What is the molecule?

3) Explain a solid object.

4) When an object is at rest, are its molecules at rest as well?

5) Until when will heat be transferred in the two bars with different temperatures?

Chapter 4-2 [Grammar Check]　名詞・冠詞・代名詞

1. 普通名詞・集合名詞・物質名詞・抽象名詞・固有名詞

9

1) I am a **student**, and they are **students,** too.
2)-1 My **family is** very large. （集合体として）
2)-2 My **family are all** early risers. （構成員に着目）
2)-3 There **are** ten **families** in the apartment house.
3) Please give me **a glass of water**.
4) **Honesty** is the best policy.
5)-1 **Abraham Lincoln** was the 16th president of **America**.
5)-2 **The Tanakas** like dogs better than cats.

---

2. 不定冠詞・定冠詞・冠詞の省略

6)-1 She waited for **an** hour.
6)-2 **A cat** can see in the dark. （総称的）
= **The cat** can see in the dark. = **Cats** can see in the dark.
7)-1 There is a book there. **The** book is written in English. （前述の名詞の指示）
7)-2 **The** earth moves around the sun. （唯一のもの）
7)-3 He likes playing **the flute**. （楽器名）
8)-1 I have **breakfast** at seven. （食事名）
cf. She had **a nice dinner** yesterday. （修飾語付き）
8)-2 We walked to **school**. （授業）　cf. We walked to **the school**. （建物）

---

3. 人称代名詞・所有代名詞・再帰代名詞・疑問代名詞・指示代名詞・不定代名詞

9) Do **you** know **her** sister?
10)-1 Is that house **yours** or **theirs**?
10)-2 She is a friend of **mine**.
11)-1 I enjoyed **myself** at the party. （再帰用法）
11)-2 He **himself** did it. （同格的に用いて強調する）
11)-3 She made the bookcase **by herself**. （慣用句）
12)-1 **Which** do you like better, this or that?
12)-2 **What** do you call your dog?
12)-3 I don't know **who she is**. （間接疑問）
13) **These** are my children. cf. Are **those cats** yours? （指示形容詞）
14)-1 **All** of the students **are** absent. cf. **All is** well with her.
14)-2 I have two sons. **One** is in Fukuoka, and **the other** is in Kyoto.
14)-3 He didn't say **anything**.
14)-4 **Each** of the students has a car.

Exercises

A. (　) 内の語を正しい形にして下線部に書きなさい.

1. Mr. White is six ________ three ________ tall.　**(foot, inch)**
2. How many ________ does this apartment house have?　**(family)**
3. Our grandfather told us a lot of interesting ________.　**(story)**
4. I have five ________ and seven ________.　**(nephew, niece)**

B. (　) 内に入る適語を下の語群から選び，正しい形にして書き入れなさい.

1. My brother drank two (　　　　　) of hot coffee this morning.
2. Bring me a (　　　　　) of red chalk, please.
3. Please put a (　　　　　) of sugar in my tea.
4. I bought two (　　　　　) of bread yesterday.

[glass / cup / loaf / piece / lump]

C. 次の文の (　) 内に適当な冠詞を入れなさい．不要な箇所には×印をつけなさい．

1. I have (　　) dinner in (　　) evening.
2. He told the helper to close (　　) window.
3. He plays (　　) tennis and she plays (　　) violin after school.
4. By (　　) way, who opened (　　) drawers?

D. 次の英文の (　) 内から適語を選びなさい.

1. I don't want this motorcycle. Do you want (it, one)?
2. Do you know (that, those) girls?
3. "(Who, Whose) is this book?" "It's my brother's."
4. He said to (his, himself), "What's the matter with her?"
5. I have two pens. One is long and (another, the other) is short.
6. (Each, Every) of the girls has her own camera.
7. (What, Which) of the books do you want to take?
8. "(Who, What) is she?" "She is a nurse."
9. (Either, Both) you or I must go there.

E. (　) 内の語を正しい形にして下線部に書きなさい.

1. She visited ________ the day before yesterday.　**(he)**
2. Is that bicycle ________ or his?　**(she)**
3. Both of ________ are dead.　**(they)**
4. Do you know ________ bicycle that is?　**(who)**
5. I bowed to him and seated ________.　**(I)**

Rearranging ▶▶▶ [　] 内の語に語頭文字が示された語を加えて並べ替え，和文に合う英文にしなさい．

1. 私の部屋には家具はあまりない． [(m　) / furniture / room / I / my / don't / in / have].

2. 彼の農場にはたくさんの牛と羊がいます．
[(s　) / lots / on / of / he / his / has / cows / farm / and].

3. それは最初から最後まで興味深い小説です．
[(e　) / is / novel / it / from / to / interesting / beginning / an].

4. 私達はそのボートを時間決め（1 時間いくら）で借りました．
[(t　) / by / the / we / hour / hired / boat].

5. 成功は勤勉な人たちのところにやって来るものだ．
[(t　) / are / come / success / who / diligent / to / will].

6. 天は自ら助くる者を助く． [(t　) / those / helps / help / who / heaven].

7. 日本の人口はフランスのそれのおよそ 2 倍である．
[(t　) / of / of / Japan / is / France / the / twice / population / about].

Basic Composition ▶▶▶ 文末の（　）内の条件をヒント（動詞は原形で提示）に英訳しなさい．

1. 彼の家族の人たちは早起きです．　(be 動詞を使い 5 語で)

2. 私のクラスの者は全員，今朝，出席している．　(class を使い 7 語で)

3. この薬を 1 日に 3 回服用しなさい．　(7 語で)

4. 地球は月よりはるかに大きい．　(far bigger を使い 8 語で)

5. この硬貨は銀でできています．　(6 語で)

6. 窓に鍵をかけないでおいたのは私です．　(it, left, unlocked を使い 8 語で)

7. 陰で他人の悪口を言うべきではない．　(ill, others, behind, backs を使い 10 語で)

8. 鶏肉の好きな人もいれば，好きでない人もいます．　(some を使い 7 語で)

Rewriting ▶▶▶ 次の各組の文がほぼ同じ意味になるように，(　) 内に適語を書き入れなさい．

1. Your shirt needs to be washed. = Your shirt needs (　　　　　　).
2. They made him go. = He was made (　　　　　　) go.
3. He didn't have less than 100,000 yen. = He had at (　　　　　　) 100,000 yen.
4. She said to me, "Thank you." = She (　　　　　　) me.
5. He cannot have done it for himself. = It is (　　　　　　) that he did it for himself.
6. I happened to meet him there. = (　　　　　　) happened that I met him there.
7. He is not so much a scholar as a teacher.
   = He is a teacher (　　　　　　) than a scholar.
8. Take an umbrella in case it rains. = Take an umbrella (　　　　　　) it should rain.
9. This will be very helpful. = This will be (　　　　　　) much help.
10. He studied hard to become a pilot.
    = He studied hard with a (　　　　　　) to becoming a pilot.

▶▶▶ Road to Science & Tech English (A4) ▶▶▶

Put into English ▶▶▶ 語句を並べ替えて，日本文に合う英文にしなさい．

1. それぞれの被覆導線の外側にマークが出るように絶縁紙を印刷すること．
   (requires printing / are formed / of each / in such a manner / covered conductor / the insulating paper / that the marks / on the outside).

   ....

2. この方法は，力が距離の２乗に反比例するという推量を検証するのに十分だった．
   (of the distance / the method / the supposition that / varies inversely / was sufficient / as the square / to verify / the force).

   ....

3. 実地調査を６回行った．1970 年と 1971 年の夏にそれぞれ３回ずつである．
   (were run / six field surveys / : / of 1970 / three / the summers / and 1971 / during / each).

   ....

The Doppler Effect

10

（ドップラー効果）

Christian Johann Doppler (1803-1853) was professor of mathematics at the technical school in Prague from 1841, and in 1851 he became professor of physics and director of the Physical Institute at the University of Vienna. He announced what has since been known as the Doppler Effect or Doppler Principle in 1848.

The horn of an approaching train at high speed seems to have a pitch higher than usual. Just as the train reaches us, the pitch of the horn suddenly drops to a much lower note. As sound waves move outward from the horn, waves moving in the same direction as the train will reach anyone standing to the front of the train with the normal speed of sound *plus* the speed of the vehicle. To the front of the train, more than the normal number of sound waves reach us per second, which causes the same effect as increasing the frequency of the sound, since frequency is measured in waves per second. An increase in frequency results in an increase in pitch. Therefore the horn of an approaching train seems to increase in pitch.

At the moment the train passes us, the sound waves now moving sidewise from the horn have only their usual speed. Therefore the frequency is lower and so is the pitch. After the train has passed us, the sound waves reach us with the normal speed of sound *minus* the speed of the train. Fewer sound waves reach us per second. This is the same as decreasing the frequency, thus lowering the pitch of the sound.

Words & Phrases: **Doppler Effect** ドップラー効果　**Christian Johann Doppler** オーストリアの物理学者・数学者　**professor of ~** ～教授（職名を表すので不定冠詞省略）　**Prague** プラハ（チェコ共和国の首都）　**director** 所長　**the Physical Institute at the University of Vienna** ウィーン大学の物理研究所　**Doppler Principle** ドップラー原理　**a pitch** 高さ cf. stress（音の強さ）　**higher than ~** 直前の a pitch にかかる　**Just as ~** ちょうど～のとき　**to a much lower note** さらに低い音へと　**sound waves** 音波　**moving** = which moves　**in the same direction as ~** ～と同じ方向に　**anyone standing to the front ~** = anyone who stands to the front ~ ～の前の方に立っている人（to が at ならば「前に」となる）　**plus** に加えて（前置詞）. cf. minus を引いた（前置詞）.　**the vehicle** = the train　**per second** = a second　**frequency** 周波数　**result in ~** 結果的に～になる Ex. His experiment resulted in a great success.（彼の実験は大成功に終わった）　**At the moment** = The moment = As soon as. 普通 at は用いない.　**the sound waves now moving ~.** = the sound waves which now moves ~.　**so is the pitch** 音の高さもそうである　**thus lowering ~** = , which thus lowers ~

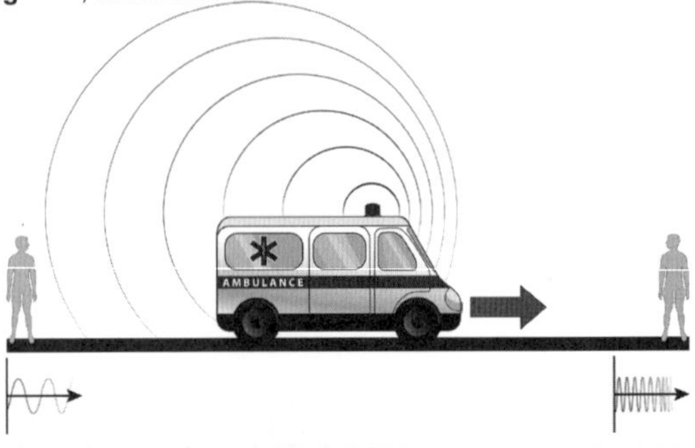

Vocabulary

語頭文字と文字数をヒントに綴りなさい.

01. 効果 e-(6字)	02. 工業の t-(9)	03. 物理学 p-(7)	04. 所長 d-(8)
05. 研究所 i-(9)	06. 発表する a-(8)	07. 警笛 h-(4)	08. 近づく a-(8)
09. 着く r-(5)	10. 突然 s-(8)	11. 外へ向かって o-(7)	12. 普通の n-(6)
13. 乗物 v-(7)	14. に加えて p-(4)	15. を引いて m-(5)	16. 秒 s-(6)
17. 周波数 f-(9)	18. 瞬間 m-(6)	19. 測定する m-(7)	20. 音の高さ p-(5)
21. 横向きに s-(8)	22. 増やす i-(8)	23. 減らす d-(8)	24. 下げる l-(5)

Q & A

1) What did Professor Doppler teach at the University of Vienna?

2) When did he announce the Doppler Effect?

3) What seems to have a pitch higher than usual?

4) Does an increase in frequency result in an increase in pitch?

5) How do the sound waves reach us after the train has passed us?

Chapter 5-2 [Grammar Check]　前置詞・接続詞（Ⅰ）

1. 前置詞

11

1) School begins **at** nine and it is over **at** four. （時の一点）
2) Turn to the right **at** the next corner. （場所の一点）
3) We have to finish the work **by** tomorrow. （期限）
4) I went from Fukuoka to Sapporo **by** plane. （交通手段）
5) He wants to work **for** world peace. （目的・追求）
6) It has been raining **for** more than five hours. （期間）
7) How far is it **from** here to your school? （起点）
8) Where do you come **from**? （出身）
9) Tom lives **in** Kyoto. （場所・位置）
10) I will be back **in** an hour. （経過時間）
11) I am a member **of** the tennis club. （所属）
12) This desk is made **of** wood. （材料）
13) There is a world map **on** the wall. （接触）
14) My father is at home **on** Sunday. （曜日・日付）
15) She went **to** France last year. （到達点）
16) We should be kind **to** old people. （関係）
17) I usually go to school **with** Akio. （同伴）
18) I have a meal **with** chopsticks. （道具）
19) They went **out of** the room. （外向運動）
20) She ran **into** the classroom. （内向運動）
21) I waited for her **till** (**until**) seven o'clock. （継続）
22) There are five bridges **over** the river. （真上）
23) The cat **under** the tree is Lucy's. （真下）
24) We remained in the bomb shelter **during** the air raid. （特定の期間中）

2. 等位接続詞 (See Ch. 13),「時」,「条件」,「原因・理由」を表す従属接続詞 (See Ch. 13)

25) Both Jack **and** Jill went to the movies yesterday.
26) He is old, **but** he is still strong.
27) Go straight on, **and** you will see the post office on your left.
28) Hurry up, **or** you will miss the train.
29) **When** he arrives home, we'll go out for dinner.
30) **If** it rains tomorrow, I won't go out.
　＊時，条件を表す副詞節では，未来のことでも現在形で表す.
31) She scolded him, **because** he told a lie.

▶▶▶ Exercises ▶▶▶

A. 次の英文の（　）内から適語を選びなさい.

1. There is a big mosquito (of, on, over) the wall.
2. Several strangers are standing (at, above, under) the gate.
3. What are you wearing (in, on, under) your coat?
4. That is a limited express bus (at, by, for) Fukuoka.
5. We chatted about the soccer game (in, on, over) coffee.

B. 次の文の（　）内に適当な前置詞を入れなさい.

1. Tires are made (　　　) rubber.
2. Taro was born (　　　) the morning of January 1.
3. He was staying (　　　) a hotel (　　　) Chicago.
4. I met her there (　　　) chance.
5. She bought a doll (　　　) twenty dollars.

C. 次の英文を日本文に直しなさい.

1. The crops are dying for want of rain.

   ……………………………………………………………………

2. Admission is free for children below the age of five.

   ……………………………………………………………………

3. In case of fire, press this button.

   ……………………………………………………………………

4. That man saved his son from drowning at the cost of his life.

   ……………………………………………………………………

5. He went out in spite of bad weather.

   ……………………………………………………………………

D.（　）内に入る適語を下の語群から選んで書き入れなさい.

1. (　　　　) he opened the door, the students stopped chatting at once.
2. (　　　　) it is fine tomorrow, we will have a barbecue in the garden.
3. He is not a teacher (　　　　) a scholar.
4. I was late (　　　　) the car broke down.
5. Hurry up, (　　　　) you can catch the 7:30 a. m. express bus.
6. I will make you lunch (　　　　) I finish cleaning.
7. Wear a warm sweater, (　　　　) you will catch cold.
8. It is true that she is young, (　　　　) she is well experienced.

[and / but / or / if / because / when / after]

Rearranging ▶▶▶ [　] 内の語に前置詞か接続詞を加えて並べ替え，和文に合う英文にしなさい．

1. 私はその絵を壁に掛けるつもりです．[（前置詞）/ the / the / hang / will / I / wall / painting].

2. 私は英国にいる間に Oxford に行った．[（前置詞）/ I / Oxford / Britain / my / in / visited / stay].

3. 彼は福岡のホテルに滞在していた．[（前置詞）/ in / hotel / a / Fukuoka / stayed / he].

4. 彼らはその計画に賛成ですか，それとも反対ですか．[（前置詞）/ are / or / against / the / they / plan]?

5. 君か私のどちらかが会合に出席しなければならない．
[（接続詞）/ to / the / you / I / meeting / attend / either / have].

6. 雨が止むまであそこで待ちましょう．[（接続詞）/ there / the / over / let's / stops / wait / rain].

7. 明日は雨が降らない限り，ハイキングに行きます．[（接続詞）/ tomorrow / will / rains / a / go / it / we / on / hike].

8. 貧しいからといって人を軽蔑してはいけない．
[（接続詞）/ he / you / despise / poor / a / not / man / is / must].

Basic Composition ▶▶▶ 文末の（　）内の条件をヒント（動詞は原形で提示）に英訳しなさい．

1. 私たちのほとんどが，折にふれてジーンズをはく．　(at one time を使い 10 語で)

2. 私の母は年の割には若く見える．　(for を使い 7 語で)

3. この花を英語で何と呼びますか．　(you を使い 8 語で)

4. 先々週，私は青森にいる叔母に手紙を書いた．　(last を使い 13 語で)

5. George は Jane にとても親切です．　(6 語で)

6. 彼は突然立ち止まった，というのも目前に大きな熊が立ちはだかったからだ．
(there, stood, ahead を使い 12 語で)

7. 春が来て，彼らは穀粒 (grain) を蒔いた．　(sowed を使い 6 語で)

8. ココナツの木 (the coconut tree) は根が (its root) 楽に水を見つけ出す (find water there) ことができるので，海の近くに育つ．　(15 語で)

Rewriting

▶▶▶ 次の各組の文がほぼ同じ意味になるように，(　) 内に適語を書き入れなさい．

1. We will go to Fukuoka by car. = We will (　　　　) to Fukuoka.
2. Tom is the tallest boy in his class. = Tom is taller than any (　　　　) boy in his class.
3. I am sorry that you didn't come to the party. = You (　　　　) have come to the party.
4. I was careless enough to let the secret out.
   = It was careless (　　　　) me to let the secret out.
5. It is clear that she came here. = (　　　　) she came here.
6. The cow supplies milk to us. = The cow supplies us (　　　　) milk.
7. There is nobody that does not love his or her country.
   = Everybody (　　　　) his or her country.
8. He said that he had returned home the previous day.
   = He said, "I returned home (　　　　)."
9. Someone knocked on the door. = (　　　　) was a knock on the door.
10. As soon as he got there, he felt sick.
    = No sooner had he got there (　　　　) he felt sick.

▶▶▶ Road to Science & Tech English (A5) ▶▶▶

Put into English

▶▶▶ 語句を並べ替えて，日本文に合う英文にしなさい．

1. 大抵のコンセントは，好奇心の強い幼児にとって都合のよいように床の近くに付いている．
   (are / of the wall, / of inquisitive children / near the floor line / electrical outlets / most / within easy reach).

2. ビー玉を糸に取り付けたように，コアをワイヤに取り付けて，ワイヤに強い電流を流すと，コアは磁化する．
   (are placed / like beads on a string, / on a wire, / if cores / through the wire, / is sent / and a strong enough electric current / become magnetized / the cores).

The Screw
（ねじ）

12

The screw is a kind of nail that has many uses. The vise on a workbench makes use of the great mechanical advantage of the screw. So does the clamp screw used to hold a piece of furniture together while it is being glued. And so do many automobile jacks and even coffee grinders in the kitchen at home.

The screw is a modification of the inclined plane. Cut a sheet of paper in the shape of a right triangle—an inclined plane. Wind it around a pencil. As the pencil is turned, the paper is wound up, so that its hypotenuse forms a spiral thread similar to the thread on a screw. The pitch of the screw, and of the paper, is the distance between any two adjacent points on the threads.

In order to understand how the screw works, consider a jack screw of the type that is used to raise a house or a piece of heavy machinery. The jack has a lever handle with a length r. If the lever handle is pulled around one turn, its outer end has described a circle. The circumference of this circle is equal to $2\pi r$. At the same time, the screw has made one revolution, and in doing so has been raised a height equal to its pitch p.

Jacks have considerable friction loss. The threads are cut so that the force used to overcome friction is greater than the force used to do useful work. If the threads were not cut this way, if no friction were present, the weight of the load would cause the jack to spin right back down to the bottom as soon as you released the handle.

Words & Phrases: **vise** 万力　**workbench** 仕事 / 作業 台　**make use of ~** ～を利用する　**the great mechanical advantage of ~** ～のすばらしい機械的な利点 / 長所　**So does the clamp screw ~** = The clamp screw（締付けねじ）makes use of the great mechanical advantage of the screw ~. 次の so do も同じ．used to の前に which is を入れて考える．　**while it is being glued** 家具がにかわで付けられている間　**automobile jacks** 自動車に使うジャッキ　**coffee grinders** コーヒーひき器　**a modification** 一つの変形　**the inclined plane** 斜面 / 傾斜面　**a right triangle** 直角三角形　**so that its hypotenuse forms a spiral thread** その結果，その直角三角形の斜辺はら線状の筋道になる．ここの thread は「ねじ山」の意味．　**similar to ~** 前に which is を補う　**the pitch of the screw** ねじのピッチ（ねじ山間の間隔をいう．紙の場合は，ここでは等間隔の筋道．　**any two adjacent points** 隣接するいかなる２点　**a lever handle with a length *r*** 長さ r のレバー・ハンドル　**is pulled around one turn** １回回される　**its outer end** レバー・ハンドルの外部先端　**circumference** 円周　**in doing so** そうするときに　**equal to** の前に which is を補って考える　**friction** 摩擦　**The threads are cut so that ~** ～であるようにねじ山が切られている　**used to**（２行目と１６行目）２つとも前に which is を入れて考える　**the weight of the load** 荷重　**cause the jack to spin right back down to ~** ぐるぐる回しながらジャッキを～まですっかり落とす原因となる．cause は使役動詞．right は副詞．Ex. *right* to the bottom すっかり底まで

Vocabulary

語頭文字と文字数をヒントに綴りなさい.

01. 利点 a-(9 字)	02. 締め具 c-(5)	03. 家具 f-(9)	04. にわかでくっつける g-(4)
05. 自動車 a-(10)	06. ジャッキ j-(4)	07. 粉砕機 g-(7)	08. 変形 m-(12)
09. 斜めになった i-(8)	10. 三角形 t-(8)	11. 巻く w-(4)	12. （直角三角形の）斜辺 h-(10)
13. らせん状の s-(6)	14. 筋道 t-(6)	15. 同様の s-(7)	16. 距離 d-(8)
17. 隣接した a-(8)	18. 上げる r-(5)	19. てこ l-(5)	20. 長さ l-(6)
21. 円周 c-(13)	22. 回転 r-(10)	23. 打ち勝つ o-(8)	24. 放す r-(7)

Q & A

1) What is the screw?

2) Does the clamp screw use the great mechanical advantage of the screw?

3) What is the distance between any two adjacent points on the threads?

4) What is the circumference of a circle with a radius (半径) of r?

5) How are the threads cut?

Chapter 6-2 [Grammar Check]　形容詞・副詞と比較級

1. 形容詞の限定・叙述用法

13

1) Alice is a **diligent** girl. （限定）　2) My uncle looks **young** for his age. （叙述）

2. 形容詞の語順（冠詞類 → 序数 → 数量 → 性状 → 大小・形状 → 色・新旧 → 材料所属）名詞

3) Would you try **these first ripe big** apples?

3. 数量形容詞

4) There are **many** / **a few** / **few** mistakes in his report.

5) We have **much** / **a little** / **little** time to decide what to do next.

4. 副詞の用法 (① 動詞・② 形容詞・③ 他の副詞を修飾)

6) Ben **studies** English very **hard**.　7) She is **very busy**.　8) He drives **too fast**.

5. 副詞の位置

・形容詞・副詞を修飾する場合：ふつう被修飾語の前

9) You're **quite** right.

・動詞を修飾する場合：① 頻度・否定・② 様態・③ 時と場所を表す副詞の場合

10)-1 She **sometimes** comes to see us. （①：一般動詞の場合はその前）

10)-2 He is **usually** free on Saturdays. （①：be 動詞・助動詞の場合はその後）

11)-1 Jill lived **happily** with Jack. （②：自動詞の場合はその後）

11)-2 She will answer the questions **easily**. （②：他動詞の場合はふつう目的語の後）

12) There was a traffic accident **here yesterday**. （③：ふつう場所の副詞が先）

6. 原級・比較級・最上級を用いた比較表現

13) She is **not as** tall **as** her sister.

14) His boat is **five times as** big **as** mine. = His boat is **five times the** size **of** mine.

15) Tom works **as** hard **as** he **can**. = Tom works **as** hard **as possible**.

16) I spent **as much** money **as** he in the amusement park yesterday.

17) Ned read **twice as many** books **as** I last month.

18) Davis is **taller than** his brother.　19) Dogs are **more useful than** cats.

20) Alice can play tennis **much better than** I. ※ 他の比較級強意語句には far, even 等。

21) There are **many more** pigs **than** people there. （複数名詞を伴って）「よりずっと多い豚」

22) Taro is **taller than any other** boy here. = Taro is **the tallest of all** the boys here.

23) Her bag is **less** heavy **than** mine. = Her bag is **not as** heavy **as** mine.

24) It is getting **colder and colder**. 「だんだん～」

25) This is **the oldest** church here.　26) Lucy is **the most beautiful** of the five.

27) She is **happiest** when she has a date with Tom. ※ 同一人 (物) に関する比較のとき the は不要.

28) He is **by far the best** here. ※ 他の強意語句: **much** (much the best), **very** (the very best)等.

29) He is **the second tallest** boy here.　30) He is **one of the most popular** actors here.

Exercises

A. 次の英文の（　）内から適語を選びなさい.

1. In Japan we have (many, much) rain in June.
2. It is raining very (hardly, hard).
3. He doesn't have (some, any) money with him.
4. There is (a few, a little) milk in the bottle.
5. Taro looks (young, younger, the youngest) than Bill.
6. Which do you like (much, well, better), tea or coffee?
7. I can't speak French as (well, better, best) as Dick.
8. He studies (hard, harder, the hardest) of the five.

B. 次の英文を［例］にならって書き換えなさい.

［例］She plays the piano very well. ⇔ She is a very good pianist.

1. Henry speaks very carefully. ⇔ ……………………
2. Betty is a very hard worker. ⇔ ……………………
3. She can speak English very well. ⇔ ……………………

C.（　）内の語を正しく並べ替えなさい.

1. (must, clean, you, your, keep, room). ……………………
2. (Bill, for, late, sometimes, is, school). ……………………
3. (kind, was, the, very, girl, us, to). ……………………
4. (an, told, story, interesting, he, us). ……………………
5. Light travels (than, much, faster) sound. ……………………
6. Mt. Fuji is (other, higher, any, than) mountain in Japan.
   ……………………
7. This is (terrible, far, the, by, most) experience I have ever had.
   ……………………
8. I want to read (many, as, as, books) I can. ……………………

D. 次の英文を日本文に直しなさい.

1. This box is five times as heavy as that one.
   ……………………
2. Come as early as possible.
   ……………………
3. He speaks English more fluently than she.
   ……………………
4. The story became more and more interesting.
   ……………………
5. This is one of the tallest buildings in the city.
   ……………………

Rearranging ▶▶▶ [　] 内の語に語頭文字が示された語を加えて並べ替え，和文に合う英文にしなさい.

1. このエンジンはどこかおかしい.
[(w　) / with / there / this / is / engine / something].

2. 当然のことながら，彼女は彼に腹を立てた. [(n　) / angry / him / she / with / got].

3. 私たちの作法のいくつかは彼らには奇妙に思われる.
[(s　) / of / are / to / some / manners / them / our].

4. 美とは, 人間の理想のひとつです. [(b　) / of / of / the / the / is / one / ideals / humans].

5. 私は彼女ほど流暢に英語を話さない. [(f　) / I / she / don't / does / as / as / English / speak].

6. 三重の人口は佐賀の人口よりも多い.
[(l　) / the / that / of / of / is / than / population / Mie / Saga].

7. その番組はますます面白くなってきている.
[(e　) / the / is / and / program / more / more / getting].

8. 彼は嘘をつくような人ではない. [(l　) / is / tell / the / a / he / man / lie / to].

Basic Composition ▶▶▶ 文末の（　）内の条件をヒント（動詞は原形で提示）に英訳しなさい.

1. あの歌の出だしはどのようですか.　(begin を使い 5 語で)

2. 幸運なことに彼は重傷ではなかった.　[(f　), (s　), (i　) を使い 6 語で]

3. 君は，きっと，すばらしい通訳になるよ.　[(s　), (g　), (i　) を使い 7 語で]

4. 金持ちが必ずしも貧乏人より幸せとは限らない.　(the, always を使い 9 語で)

5. 私の両親はもはや生きてはいない.　(longer を使い 6 語で)

6. 彼は千円しか持っていない.　(more を使い 8 語で)

7. 私は彼を知れば知るほど彼が嫌いになった.　(more, less, liked を使い 10 語で)

8. 彼は自由な時間を最大限に利用した.　(made, most を使い 8 語で)

Rewriting ▶▶▶ 次の各組の文がほぼ同じ意味になるように，(　) 内に適語を書き入れなさい．

1. He is an English teacher at this school. = He (　　　　　) English at this school.
2. You should see the musical. = (　　　　　) don't you see the musical?
3. Who broke the window? = Who was the window broken (　　　　　)?
4. It is no use trying to do that. = It is (　　　　　) to try to do that.
5. He said, "No." = He answered in the (　　　　　).
6. He found ten mistakes in ten lines. = He found ten mistakes in as (　　　　　) lines.
7. Without music, the world would be dull.
   = If (　　　　　) were not for music, the world would be dull.
8. She was a beauty in her day. = She was beautiful when she was (　　　　　).
9. Be it ever so humble, home is home.
   = (　　　　　) humble it may be, home is home.
10. My house is five minutes' walk from here.
    = It (　　　　　) five minutes to walk to my house from here.

▶▶▶ Road to Science & Tech English (A6) ▶▶▶

Put into English ▶▶▶ 語句を並べ替えて，日本文に合う英文にしなさい．

1. 使用するスポンジは濡れている方が良いが，びしょぬれの状態であってはならない．落ちるしずくは最小にすること．
   (minimize dripping / the sponge / keep / used wet / and / but / not soaked).

   ....

2. 地上の大気中の水蒸気の含有量は高さによって変化することが多い．この変化は，電波に対して著しい導波効果をもたらす．
   In (with the height / above the earth's surface / often varies / the atmosphere / the moisture / vapor content). (a pronounced / upon / causes / guiding effect / this variation / radio waves).

   ....

3. イオウを除いた多くの鉱物は，海底にあまり硬くかたまらずに堆積しているので，浚渫機で採取できる．
   (are found / are recovered / many minerals, / by dredgers / except sulfur, / and / on the sea floor, / in unconsolidated / deposits).

   ....

Gears

(ギヤ)

14

Gears are used in many machines. Frequently the gears are hidden from view in a protective case filled with grease or oil.

When two shafts are not lying in the same straight line, but are parallel, motion can be transmitted from one to the other by means of spur gears. Spur gears are wheels with mating teeth cut in their surfaces so that one can turn the other without slippage. When the mating teeth are cut so that they are parallel to the axis of rotation, the gears are called straight spur gears.

When two gears of unequal size are meshed together, the smaller of the two is usually called a pinion. An unequal number of teeth causes one gear to be of a larger diameter than the other. The teeth themselves must be of the same size in order to mesh properly.

The most commonly used type are the straight spur gears, but another type of spur gears, the helical spur gear is also widely used. In helical gears the teeth are cut slantwise across the working face of the gear. One end of the tooth, therefore, lies ahead of the other. In other words, each tooth has a leading end and a trailing end. In the straight spur gears the whole width of the teeth comes in contact at the same time. But with helical gears contact between two teeth starts first at the leading ends and moves progressively across the gear faces until the trailing ends are in contact. This kind of meshing action keeps the gears in constant contact with one another.

Words & Phrases: **are hidden from view** 隠れて見えない **in a protective case** 保護ケースに（入っていて） (which is) **filled with ~** ～が一杯入った **are not lying in the same straight line, but ~** （２本のシャフトが）１本の直線上になくて，～ならば（not ~ but の構文） **be transmitted from one** (shaft) **to the other** (shaft) **by means of spur gears** 平歯車によって１本のシャフトから他のシャフトへ伝達される **mating teeth** かみ合う相手となる歯 (which are) **cut in their surfaces** それぞれの周りに切られた **without slippage** すべることなく **the axis of rotation** 回転軸 **straight spur gears** 直刃平歯車 **are meshed together** お互いにかみ合う **pinion** 小歯車 cf. gear wheel 大歯車 **helical spur gear** はすば平歯車 **slantwise across the working face of the gear** ギアの作動面を斜めに **lies ahead of the other** (end) 他の端の先にある **has a leading end and a trailing end** 前端と後端がある **the whole width of the teeth** 歯車の全歯幅 **progressively** = gradually 徐々に **the gear faces** 歯先面

Vocabulary

語頭文字と文字数をヒントに綴りなさい.

01. しばしば f-(10字)	02. 保護用の p-(10)	03. 丸棒 s-(5)	04. 平行な p-(8)
05. 伝える t-(8)	06. 手段 m-(5)	07. 滑ること s-(8)	08. かみ合う ma-(4)
09. 軸 a-(4)	10. 回転 r-(8)	11. 真っ直ぐな s-(8)	12. 小歯車 p-(6)
13. 不等の u-(7)	14. 直径 d-(8)	15. かみ合う me-(4)	16. 適当に p-(8)
17. 先立つ l-(7)	18. らせんの h-(7)	19. 斜めに s-(9)	20. 後端の t-(8)
21. 幅 w-(5)	22. 徐々に p-(13)	23. 不断の c-(8)	24. 軸に平行に歯を切った s-(4)

Q & A

1) Where are the gears frequently hidden from view?

2) What are spur gears?

3) What are the gears called when the mating teeth are cut so that they are parallel to the axis of rotation?

4) Are the straight spur gears used more commonly than the helical spur gears?

5) Where does first contact between two teeth start in helical gears?

Chapter 7-2 [Grammar Check] 命令文・感嘆文

15

1. 命令文

1) **Look** at the map of the city of Rome.
2) **Be** quiet here.
3) Waiter, please **give** me a cup of coffee.
4) **Don't speak** Japanese in this room.
5) **Don't be** late for school again.
6) **Let** me know where he lives.
7) **Let's** toss a coin to decide.
8) **Get up** early, **or** you will miss the train.
9) **Turn** to the right, **and** you will find the school.
10) **Let's not** talk about it.

2. What 感嘆文

11) **What a wonderful city** Rome is!
12) **What an interesting book** this is!
13) **What lovely flowers** those are!
14) **What wonderful hair** she has!
15) **What a waste**!　「何ともったいないことか」
16) **What a shame**!　「何と残念なことか」
17) **What a terrible thing** to do!　「何とひどいことをすることか」
18) **What luck**!　「何と運がいいことか」
19) **What nonsense**!　「何とばかばかしいことか」

3. How 感嘆文

20) **How foolish** I was!
21) **How beautifully** she is singing!
22) **How boring** his lectures are!
23) **How wonderful a city** Rome is!
24) **How careless** of you to do so!　「そんなことをするなんて，何と不注意なことか」
25) **How kind** of you to say so!　「そう言ってくれてありがとう」
26) **How** he has grown!　「何と大きくなったことか」
27) **How** she talks!　「何とよくしゃべることか」
28) **How it snows** here in winter!　「何と雪が多いことか」

Exercises

A. 次の英文を命令文にしなさい.

1. You are silent here. ……………………
2. You don't mix these together. ……………………
3. You will be back here by eleven o'clock. ……………………
4. We will play tennis after school. ……………………
5. We will not go there. ……………………

B. 次の英文を感嘆文にしなさい.

1. That is a very amusing story. ……………………
2. These are very interesting books. ……………………
3. The athlete is running very fast. ……………………
4. You look very pale. ……………………
5. You have very good pictures. ……………………
6. It is very foolish of you to do such a thing. ……………………

C. 次の日本文を(　)内の語句を使って英文に直しなさい.

1. 私にもっと食べ物をください. (please, food)

……………………

2. 泣くな. 手伝うから. (cry, help)

……………………

3. ドライブに行こう. (a drive)

……………………

4. 君は何と素敵な本を書いたことか. (nice, written)

……………………

5. 君は何と美しいバラを持っていることか. (roses)

……………………

6. これは何と古い切手だこと. (old stamp)

……………………

7. その花は何といい香りがすることか. (smells)

……………………

8. 風は何と強く吹くことか. (blow hard)

……………………

9. 彼は何と利口なことか. (clever)

……………………

Rearranging ▶▶▶ （　）内の語に１語加えて並べ替え，和文に合う英文にしなさい．

1. Ann は何とすぐれた運動選手なのでしょう．　(is / fine / an / Ann / athlete)!

2. 彼女たちは何と親切な少女たちだろう．　(girls / are / kind / they)!

3. 彼の身なりは何と滑稽だったことか．　(clothes / were / ridiculous / his)!

4. 彼は私に何と難しい質問をしたことか．　(difficult / asked / a / me / question / he)!

5. 学校に遅れてはいけません．　(be / for / school / late).

6. 来週の金曜日にパーティーを開きましょう．　(next / have / party / Friday / a).

7. 他人をからかうのをよしましょう．　(others / make / of / let's / fun).

8. この川では絶対に一人で泳ぐな．　(swim / this / in / river / never).

Basic Composition ▶▶▶ 文末の（　）内の条件をヒント（動詞は原形で提示）に英訳しなさい．

1. 弱者に親切でやさしくありなさい．　(be, to を使い 7 語で)

2. あまり長くビデオゲームをしてはならない．　(a, very を使い 7 語で)

3. すぐに起きなさい，さもないと置いてけぼりにするよ．(once, we'll without を使い 9 語で)

4. しばらく休憩を取りましょう．　(let's, while を使い 7 語で)

5. 今夜その会合に出席するのはやめましょう．　(let's を使い 6 語で)

6. 昌子ははなんと流暢に英語を話せるのでしょう．　(fluently を使い 6 語で)

7. あれは何と長い橋なのでしょう．　(6 語で)

8. 子供たちは上の部屋で何と大騒ぎをしているのでしょう．
(big, noise, upper を使い 12 語で)

Rewriting ▶▶▶ 次の各組の文がほぼ同じ意味になるように，（　）内に適語を書き入れなさい．

1. When he was twenty, he became an actor.
   =He became an actor (　　　　　　) the age of twenty.
2. This water is so clean as to drink. = This water is clean (　　　　　　) to drink.
3. He said that he would leave there the next day.
   = He said, "I will leave here (　　　　　　)."
4. Why didn't you come? = (　　　　　　) prevented you from coming?
5. He is helping his mother. = His mother is being (　　　　　　) by him.
6. I don't know what to do. = I don't know what I (　　　　　　) do.
7. By whom was this picture taken? = Who (　　　　　　) this picture?
8. She married an old man. = She got married (　　　　　　) an old man.
9. He discussed the problem earnestly.
   = He discussed the problem (　　　　　　) earnest.
10. He is a very fast runner. = (　　　　　　) a fast runner he is!

▶▶▶ Road to Science & Tech English (A7) ▶▶▶

Put into English ▶▶▶ 語句を並べ替えて，日本文に合う英文にしなさい．

1. ネジは釘よりも高価で，しかも，ねじ込むのが大変だが，釘にない特長をもっているため，多くの仕事に理想的である．
   (are more expensive / are more difficult / make them / for many projects / screws / but / than / to drive, / ideal / special characteristics / nails and).

   ....

   ....

2. 今日まで宇宙に打ち上げられたすべてのロケットは普通の化学燃料で推進されるもので，多段式の原則によるものである．
   (by / on / all the rockets / the multistage principle / so far / and based / sent into space / ordinary chemical fuel / have been propelled).

   ....

   ....

Types of Clutches

（いろいろな型のクラッチ）

16

A clutch is a form of coupling which is designed to connect or disconnect a driving and a driven member for stopping or starting the driven part. There are two general classes of clutches—positive clutches and friction clutches.

Positive Clutches. Positive clutches have teeth which interlock. The simplest is the jaw or claw type, which is usable only at low speeds. The spiral claw or ratchet type cannot be reversed. An example of a clutch is seen in bicycles—it engages the rear sprocket with the rear wheel when the pedals are pushed forward, and lets the rear wheel revolve freely when the pedals are stopped.

Friction Clutches. The object of a friction clutch is to connect a rotating member to one that is stationary, to bring it up to speed, and to transmit power with a minimum of slippage. A cone clutch is commonly used in motor trucks. In autos a disc clutch is used. A disc clutch may also have a number of plates. Single-disc clutches are frequently dry clutches (no lubrication); multiple-disc clutches may be dry or wet (lubricated).

Magnetic clutches are a recent development in which the friction surfaces are brought together by magnetic force when the electricity is turned on. Rim clutches are named according to the way the pressure is applied to the rim-block, split-ring, band, or roller.

Coil clutches are used where heavy parts are to be moved, as in a rolling mill.

Pneumatic and hydraulic clutches are used on Diesel engines and transportation equipment.

Words & Phrases: **clutches** クラッチ（2つの軸の一方から他方へ，任意に断続して動力を伝達する装置） **coupling** = joint 継手 **a driving** (member) **and a driven member** = 駆動要素と駆動される要素（駆動・被駆動部） **positive clutches** 確実クラッチ（一方が動けば , 相手は壊れない限り必ず動くクラッチ） **friction clutches** 摩擦クラッチ（摩擦を利用して運動を断続させるクラッチ） **have teeth which interlock** 噛み合う歯がついている **the jaw or claw type** あご，即ち，かぎつめ型 **The spiral claw or ratchet type** らせん状のつめ，即ち，ラチェット型（フランジ flange 面のつめ claw を噛み合わせて回転を伝達するクラッチ．噛み合うときだけ回転力が伝わる． **it engages the rear sprocket with the rear wheel** クラッチで後部スプロケットと後輪が噛み合う（sprocket は鎖車ともいう．） **with a minimum of slippage** 最少のすべりで **cone clutch** 円錐クラッチ（円錐面の摩擦により回転を伝えるクラッチ．cone / conical friction clutch ともいう．） **motor trucks** = trucks 貨物自動車 **disc clutch** 円板クラッチ（円板面を摩擦面としたクラッチ．） **a number of plates** 数多くの板 **single-disc clutches** 単板クラッチ（single plate clutch ともいう．） **dry clutches** 乾式クラッチ（opp. wet 湿式な．） **no lubrication** 潤滑しない **multiple-disc clutch** 多板クラッチ **magnetic clutches** 磁気クラッチ（磁気力 magnetic force を利用して，2軸の連結を行うクラッチ） **rim clutches** リム・クラッチ（ひろげクラッチ expanding clutch ともいう．） **the rim-block, split-ring, band, or roller** リムの機構，割りリング，帯，ローラー **coil clutches** コイル・クラッチ **rolling mill** 圧延機（金属素材を加熱して型材を作る機械．） **pneumatic and hydraulic clutches** 空気クラッチや水圧クラッチ **transportation equipment** 輸送車両

Vocabulary

語頭文字と文字数をヒントに綴りなさい.

01. 接続する c-(7字)	02. 切断する d-(10)	03. 一般的な g-(7)	04. 確実動作の p-(8)
05. 噛み合う i-(9)	06. あご j-(3)	07. かぎづめ c-(4)	08. 使用できる u-(6)
09. らせん状の s-(6)	10. 歯止め装置 r-(7)	11. 逆進させる r-(7)	12. 噛み合わせる e-(6)
13. 後部の r-(4)	14. 鎖歯車 s-(8)	15. 回転する r-(7)	16. 目的 o-(6)
17. 回転する r-(6)	18. 静止している s-(10)	19. 伝える t-(8)	20. 潤滑 l-(11)
21. 空気の p-(9)	22. 水圧の h-(9)	23. 輸送 t-(14)	24. 車両 e-(9)

Q & A

1) What is a clutch?

2) How many general kinds of clutches are there?

3) What is the object of a friction clutch?

4) How are the friction surfaces brought together?

5) Where are coil clutches used?

Chapter 8-2 [Grammar Check] 不定詞

17

1. 不定詞の基本的用法

・名詞的用法

1) **To smoke** here is not allowed. （主語として）

2) I want **to travel** abroad. （目的語として）

3) My dream is **to help** sick and poor people. （補語として）

・形容詞的用法

4) I have some friends **to support** me.

5) There is no one **to help** the greedy man in the world.

6) I want something **to drink**.

・副詞的用法

7) I got up early **to catch** the first train. （目的）

8) I am glad **to hear** the news. （原因・理由）

9) He awoke **to find** himself in a strange room. （結果）

2. 不定詞に関する基本事項および慣用表現

10) It is good for the health **to keep** early hours. （形式主語によって文尾に）

11) I found it difficult **to solve** the problem. （形式目的語によって文尾に）

12) Dave often **asks** me **to help** him with his homework. （目的語＋不定詞）
= Dave often says to me, "Please help me with my homework."

13) Do you know **what to do** next? （疑問詞＋不定詞）
= Do you know what you should do next?

14) She was **too tired to walk** any farther.
= She was so tired that she couldn't walk any farther.

15) He is tall **enough to touch** the ceiling.
= He is so tall that he can touch the ceiling.

16) He told me **not to open** the door. （不定詞の否定）
= He said to me, "Don't open the door."

17) I never **heard** him **sing**. （知覚動詞の後の原形不定詞）
→ He was never heard **to sing** by me.

18) They **made** me **work** all day long. （使役動詞の後の原形不定詞）
→ I was made **to work** all day long.

19) You don't have to go there if you don't want **to**. （代不定詞）
= You don't have to go there if you don't want **to go there**.

20) You **had better** start at once. 「～するほうがいい」

Exercises

A. 次の英文を日本文にしなさい.

1. There was no time to lose.
2. To get up early, you must go to bed early.
3. I found it difficult to do so.
4. Will you lend me something to write with?
5. He was very disappointed to hear the result.

B. 次の１～３の文中の不定詞と同じ用法のものを下から２つずつ選び，記号で答えなさい．

1. His only fault is to talk too much. (　　) (　　)
2. Please give me something to drink. (　　) (　　)
3. I was surprised to hear the news of his death. (　　) (　　)

a) Please come to see us next Sunday.　b) He has no house to live in.
c) Please teach me how to cook.　d) It is my great pleasure to read books after supper.
e) He grew up to be a great scientist.　f) The best way to master English is practice.

C. 次の各組の文がほぼ同じ意味になるように，(　) 内に適語を書き入れなさい.

1. They saw her wash the dishes. = She was (　　　　) (　　　　) wash the dishes.
2. She said to her son, "Don't swim in the river."
   = She told her son (　　　　) (　　　　) swim in the river.
3. He is so rich that he can buy a yacht. = He is rich (　　　　) (　　　　) buy a yacht.
4. The dress is so expensive that she cannot buy it.
   = The dress is (　　　　) expensive (　　　　) her (　　　　) buy.

D. 次の日本文を (　) 内の語句を使って英文に直しなさい.

1. 私はそれを聞いてとてもうれしい.（glad, hear that）
2. 彼の仕事はバスを運転することです.（job, drive）
3. この部屋には座る椅子がありません.（no chairs, on）
4. この英和辞典は使い易いです.（easy, use）

Rearranging

(　　) 内の語に 1 語加えて並べ替え，和文に合う英文にしなさい．

1. 彼は私にこの部屋を使わないように言った．　(me / to / he / room / told / use / this).
2. この小説は 1 日で読めるほど短い．　(is / to / one / this / short / day / novel / read / in).
3. 彼女は私に 1 時間後に戻ってくると約束した．　(me / in / she / hour / to / an / back / be).
4. 秋は読書に最良の季節です．　(is / read / the / to / season / best).
5. 出かける前に窓を閉めるのを忘れないように．
   (to / leaving / don't / window / close / before / the).
6. 切符をどこで買えばよいのか教えて下さい．　(tell / buy / please / ticket / me / a / to).
7. そんなことをするなんて，彼は狂っているに違いない．
   (he / mad / a / must / thing / be / do / to).
8. 彼は電車に乗り遅れたようだ．　(the / to / missed / he / train / seems).
9. 彼女は外国に行ってしまったと思われた．　(abroad / was / she / to / gone / have).
10. 何か冷たい飲み物をください．　(me / cold / to / please / drink / give).

Basic Composition

文末の (　) 内の条件をヒント (動詞は原形で提示) に英訳しなさい．

1. 最寄のコンビニにはどうやって行けばよいのか教えていただけませんか．
   (could, get を使用して 12 語で)
2. 急ぐ必要はありません．　(there, no, be を使用して 9 語で)
3. 私はスキーに行ったが，脚を折っただけだった．　(, only を使用して 8 語で)
4. 言うまでもなくそのバスは遅れた．　(needless を使用して 7 語で)
5. 早寝早起きは健康によい．　(it, keep を使用して 10 語で)
6. 君が禁煙するのは無理だろう．　(it, will, impossible, give を使用して 10 語で)
7. その知らせを聞いて彼らは喜んだ．　(made を使用して 5 語で)

Rewriting ▶▶▶ 次の各組の文がほぼ同じ意味になるように，( ) 内に適語を書き入れなさい.

1. There are seven days in a week. = A week ( ) seven days.
2. Mary did not say anything to me. = Mary said ( ) to me.
3. He is anything but a fool. = He is ( ) fool.
4. His novel is not interesting at all. = His novel is ( ) from interesting.
5. He ran away so as not to be seen.
   = He ran away so ( ) he might not be seen.
6. You may have it if only you ask for it. = You may have it ( ) the asking.
7. The exam is too difficult for me to pass.
   = The exam is so difficult that I can't pass ( ).
8. May I lie on the sofa? = Would you ( ) my lying on the sofa?
9. Small boy as he was, he lifted the barrel.
   = ( ) he was a small boy, he lifted the barrel.
10. I think it is better for you to do so. = You ( ) better do so.

▶▶▶ Road to Science & Tech English (A8) ▶▶▶

Put into English ▶▶▶ 語句を並べ替えて，日本文に合う英文にしなさい.

1. 金属は良導体である．物体の中には頑固に絶縁体のままでいるものもある．半導体と呼ばれる第三種の物質は，非常に微小な不純物を含むと電気を通す.

   (are / of electricity / metals / good conductors). (consistently / insulators / some substances / remain). (a third class / called semiconductors, / can conduct electricity / of materials, / when they / quantities / certain impurities / very minute / contain / in).

2. アパートの水道管はアース系統の一部であるので，コーヒポットや電気炊飯器などのような電気器具のコードをコンセントに差し込んだまま洗うのは極めて危険である.

   (because / the electrical "ground" system, / of apartments / the water piping / is part of / an electric rice cooker, etc. / it is / to wash a coffee pot and / extremely dangerous / still connected / with the appliance / to the electrical outlet).

The Combustion Engine

（燃焼機関）

18

An engine is defined simply as a machine that converts heat energy to mechanical energy. Combustion is the act of burning. Internal means inside or enclosed. Thus an internal combustion engine is one in which the fuel burns inside; that is, burning takes place within the same cylinder that produces energy to turn the crankshaft. In external combustion engines, such as steam engines, the combustion takes place outside the engine.

The external combustion engine requires a boiler to which heat is applied. This combustion causes water to boil to produce steam. The steam passes into the engine cylinder under pressure and forces the piston to move downward. With the internal combustion engine, the combustion takes place inside the cylinder and is directly responsible for forcing the piston to move downward.

The transformation of heat energy to mechanical energy by the engine is based on a fundamental law of physics which states that gas will expand upon application of heat. The law also states that when a gas is compressed the temperature of the gas will increase. If the gas is confined with no outlet for expansion, then the pressure of the gas will be increased when heat is applied. In an engine, this pressure acts against the head of a piston, causing it to move downward.

All internal combustion engines, whether gasoline or diesel, are basically the same. They all rely on three things—air, fuel, and ignition. All are essential, and the engine will not operate if any one of them is missing.

Words & Phrases: **combustion engine** 燃焼機関（内燃機関 **internal -** と外燃機関 **external -** とがある） **is defined simply as ~** 簡単に～と定義される **converts heat energy to mechanical energy** 熱エネルギーを機械エネルギーに変える **energy** エネルギー（仕事をなしうる能力） **one** = engine **take place** 起こる **the same cylinder** 同一のシリンダー **crankshaft** クランク軸（往復運動を回転運動に変える装置） **steam engines** 蒸気機関（ボイラーで発生した蒸気の膨張力を利用してピストンに往復運動を起こさせて動力を得る機関.） **causes water to boil to produce steam** 水を沸騰させて蒸気を作る **the engine cylinder under pressure** 圧力の働いている機関のシリンダー **forces the piston to move downward** ピストンを強制的に下方へ動かす **is directly responsible for ~** 直接～の一因となる **the transportation of heat energy to ~** 熱エネルギーを～に変えること **is based on a fundamental law of physics** 物理学の基本法則に基づいている **gas will expand upon application of heat** 気体は加熱すると膨張する **a gas is compressed** 気体が圧縮される **is confined with no outlet for expansion** 膨張の為の出口がなく閉じ込められる **acts against the head of a piston** ピストンヘッドの運動に逆らう **ignition** 点火

Vocabulary

語頭文字と文字数をヒントに綴りなさい.

01. 定義する d-(6字)	02. 変える c-(7)	03. 内部の i-(8)	04. 囲む e-(7)
05. 燃焼する b-(4)	06. 燃料 f-(4)	07. クランク軸 c-(10)	08. 外部の e-(8)
09. ボイラー b-(6)	10. 加える a-(5)	11. 原因となる r-(11)	12. 強いてさせる f-(5)
13. 変化 t-(14)	14. 基本の f-(11)	15. 圧縮する c-(8)	16. 閉じ込める c-(7)
17. 出口 o-(6)	18. 圧力 p-(8)	19. 燃焼 c-(10)	20. 作動する o-(7)
21. 基本的に b-(9)	22. 点火 i-(8)	23. 不可欠の e-(9)	24. 欠ける m-(7)

Q & A

1) How is an engine defined?

2) In an internal combustion engine, where does burning take place?

3) What is the piston forced to move downward by?

4) What will happen when a gas is compressed?

5) What do all internal combustion engines concretely rely on?

Chapter 9-2 [Grammar Check] 動名詞と分詞

動名詞

19

1. 文の主要素（主語，補語，目的語）

1) **Seeing** is believing.
2) My hobby is **collecting** stamps.
3) Her brother stopped **smoking** two months ago. cf. I stopped to smoke.（修飾語）
4) I like **swimming**. cf. I like to swim.（「～したい」と一時的な場合もある）
5) **It** is no use **crying** over spilt milk. (It = crying ...)

2. 前置詞の目的語

6) We usually begin class by **reviewing** the last lesson.
7) How about **going** on a picnic?
8) I'm looking forward to **seeing** you soon.

3. 名詞を修飾 …「名詞 for 動名詞」と解釈

9) This is a **sleeping** car. (= a car for sleeping)
10) He happened to meet her in the **waiting** room.
11) She got a can of orange juice from the **vending** machine.

4. 動名詞を目的語にとる動詞

12) You should **practice speaking** English every day.
13) I **missed watching** the TV program last night.
14) He **suggested playing** outside.
= He suggested that we should play outside.
※ 他に、admit, avoid, enjoy, escape, finish, mind, put off, stop など

現在分詞と過去分詞

1. 分詞の限定用法（前置と後置）

15)-1 A **drowning** man will catch at a straw.
15)-2 A **lost** chance will never come again.
16)-1 Who is the girl **standing** next to Della?
16)-2 The dinner **cooked** by Father was very delicious.

2. 分詞の叙述用法 (主格補語・目的格補語として)

17)-1 Dick stood **talking** with Beth in the train.
17)-2 He looked **worried** about his health.
18)-1 I saw him **watering** the flowers.
18)-2 I heard my name **called**.

Exercises

A. (　) 内の語を動名詞か分詞に変え，下線部に書き入れなさい．

1. They enjoyed _________ a baseball game on TV. **(watch)**
2. There is no _________ room in this building. **(smoke)**
3. Her job is _________ vegetables. **(sell)**
4. She is good at _________ the guitar. **(play)**
5. My son went out without _________ good-by. **(say)**
6. Who is that _________ boy? **(cry)**
7. There is a _________ watch on the desk. **(break)**
8. Look at the boy _________ in the river. **(swim)**
9. I have a car _________ in Germany. **(make)**
10. The dog came _________ across the street. **(run)**

B. (　) 内の語句を正しく並べ替えなさい．

1. My (hear / surprised / news / father / the / looked / to).
2. We (looking / for / at / remained / other / a / each) while.
3. There (standing / the doorway / is / in / someone).
4. You (be / water / the / careful / boiling / must / with).
5. The (my father's / is / by / washed / car / Tom).
6. (a letter / is / easy / in English / writing / not).
7. My (model planes / hobby / brother's / making / is).
8. (working / of / with / the / she / famous / proud / architect / is).

C. 次の日本文を (　) 内の語句を使って英文に直しなさい．

1. 彼は私にフランス語で書かれた手紙を見せた．(showed)
2. 私は夕食前に宿題をし終えました．(doing, dinner)
3. 彼女はあなたから便りをもらうことを楽しみに待っています．(looking, hearing)

Rearranging ▶▶▶ (　　) 内の語に 1 語加えて並べ替え，和文に合う英文にしなさい.

1. 彼らは全員たのしく試合を観戦した.　(the / all / game / enjoyed / they).

2. 彼は私がそこへ行くべきだと言い張った.　(me / there / he / going / insisted).

3. この湖で泳ぐ際は気をつけなさい.　(in / in / be / lake / careful / this).

4. 彼のことを気の毒に思わざるをえない.　(for / I / him / sorry / cannot / feeling).

5. その事実を否定できない.　(the / there / denying / is / fact).

6. 劇場で財布を盗まれました.　(I / my / in / had / the / wallet / theater).

7. 長く待たせ続けてご免なさい.　(I'm / you / have / long / kept / to / sorry).

8. 大変疲れを感じたので，ひと休みした.　(tired, / I / rest / a / very / took).

9. 天候が許せば，今週末体育祭があります.
(have / day / this / we / sports / weather / will / weekend, / a).

Basic Composition ▶▶▶ 文末の ( ) 内の条件をヒント（動詞は原形で提示）に英訳しなさい.

1. あの空高く飛んでいる鳥を見て下さい.　(look, up を使用して 10 語で)

2. 彼等は落ち葉を道端に掃き寄せている.　(side, road を使用して 11 語で)

3. 私は幼年期に車にはねられたことを覚えている.　(hit, my を使用して 10 語で)

4. その本を取っていただけませんか.　(mind, handing を使用して 7 語で)

5. お出でいただけないのは残念です.　(it, disappointing, me を使用して 8 語で)

6. 何と言ってよいかわからなかったので, 彼は黙っていた. (knowing, kept を使用して 8 語で)

7. その日は天気がよかったので, 私たちはハイキングに行った. (being, を使用して 7 語で)

8. 一般的に言って，早起きは三文の得.　(generally, catches を使用して 8 語で)

9. 私たちは黒のネクタイをして葬式に出る.　(attend, wearing を使用して 8 語で)

Rewriting ▶▶▶ 次の各組の文がほぼ同じ意味になるように，（　）内に適語を書き入れなさい．

1. He didn't go to school yesterday. = He was absent (　　　　　　) school yesterday.
2. All the angles of a triangle are under 180°.
   = All the angles of a triangle are (　　　　　　) than 180°.
3. He said to me, "Will you come to my party?" = He (　　　　　　) me to his party.
4. Business brought him to Japan. = He came to Japan (　　　　　　) business.
5. When he saw a policeman, he ran away.
   = (　　　　　　) the sight of a policeman, he ran away.
6. He would often be late for school.
   = As was often the (　　　　　　) with him, he was late for school.
7. Not a soul was to be seen in the park.
   = Not a soul (　　　　　　) be seen in the park.
8. There is no rule that has no exceptions. = All rules (　　　　　　) some exceptions.
9. He solved the problem with ease. = He solved the problem (　　　　　　).
10. The boy who is standing over there is my cousin.
    = The boy (　　　　　　) over there is my cousin.

▶▶▶ Road to Science & Tech English (A9) ▶▶▶

Put into English ▶▶▶ 語句を並べ替えて，日本文に合う英文にしなさい．

1. 大抵の自転車には，反射鏡はオプションでなく普通のものとして付いております．ランプは夜乗るには必要欠くべからざるものですが，昼間しか利用しない自転車なら，反射鏡もランプも必要ありません．
   (with reflectors / most bicycles / as a standard item / are equipped). (at night, / lights / for bicycling / are essential / but reflectors and lights / only during daylight hours / if the bicycle / are not necessary / is used).

   ……………………………………………………………………………………

   ……………………………………………………………………………………

2. 血圧は電気信号として非常に細い線によって読み出され，ブラウン管，または，記録紙に表示される．
   Blood pressures (as electrical signals / and displayed / are read out / or recorded / through very fine wires / on the cathode-ray tube) on the paper.

   ……………………………………………………………………………………

   ……………………………………………………………………………………

The Thermostat

（サーモスタット）

20

The amount of heat is controlled automatically in certain electrical devices by means of a thermostat, which is a switch that automatically turns power to the element on and off to keep its temperature stable within just a few degrees.

The heart of all thermostats is a bimetal blade, a strip of metal made from two unlike alloys, one with a high rate of expansion when heated, and the other with a low rate. When heated, the high-expansion metal is "held" by the one with a low expansion rate, and the combination of forces causes the blade to bend. When the heat is removed, the blade returns to its normally straight position. This action can be used to control the heat from an electric heater. This is done by placing the bimetal blade where the heat from the main heating element will raise its temperature. When the heat rises above a predetermined level, the blade bends, opening the contact; and the heating element cools off. When the temperature of the blade drops to a lower limit, the blade straightens out once more, closing the contact; and the heating element goes on again. This process is repeated constantly while the appliance is on.

By altering the proportion and alloy of the two metals in the blade, thermostats can be designed to give almost any desired temperature control. In precision applications they can be made so sensitive that the temperature is kept constant to within one degree. Ordinary appliance thermostats do not have to be quite so sensitive.

Words & Phrases: **thermostat** サーモスタット（一定の温度を保たせるための装置） **by means of ~** ～の手段により **turns power ~ on and off** ～に電気を入れたり切ったりする **to the element** 発熱体 / 素子へ **keep ~ stable** ～を安定させ続ける **a bimetal blade** バイメタル・ブレード（bi- は 2 つを意味し，blade は薄く平たいもののこと．bimetal は二枚の熱膨張係数の異なる金属板のこと． **strip** 細片 **unlike alloys** 異なった合金 **a high rate of expansion** 膨張率の大きい **when heated** = when it is heated **a low rate** = a low rate of expansion **is "held" by ~** ～により押さえられる **the combination of forces** この力の結合（により） **an electric heater** 電熱器（電気コンロ **hot plate** ではなく．もっと範囲が広く，料理，暖房，温水，その他工業，農業にも利用される． **the heat from the main heating element** 主要発熱体から出る熱 **opening the contact** = and it opens the contact **cools off** 冷たくなる **goes on again** 再び電気が入る **while the appliance is on** 機械に電気が入っている間中 **the proportion and alloy of ~** ～の割合と合金 **in precision applications** 精密に用いられると

Vocabulary

語頭文字と文字数をヒントに綴りなさい.

01.	装置	d-(6字)	02.	電気の	e-(10)	03.	自動的に	a-(13)	04.	温度自動調整器	t-(10)
05.	安定した	s-(6)	06.	ブレード	b-(5)	07.	細片	s-(5)	08.	異なった	u-(6)
09.	膨張	e-(9)	10.	曲がる	b-(4)	11.	取り除く	r-(6)	12.	通常	n-(8)
13.	真っ直ぐな	s-(8)	14.	電気の	e-(8)	15.	設定されている	p-(13)	16.	真っ直ぐになる	s-(10)
17.	電気器具	a-(9)	18.	変える	a-(5)	19.	割合	p-(10)	20.	合金	a-(5)
21.	望み通りの	d-(7)	22.	精密	p-(9)	23.	一定の	c-(8)	24.	敏感な	s-(9)

Q & A

1) What is a thermostat?

2) What is a bimetal blade made from?

3) When does the blade return to its normally straight position?

4) How can thermostats be designed to give almost any desired temperature control?

5) Can thermostats be made sensitive enough for the temperature to be kept constant to within one degree when they are precisely applied?

Chapter 10-2 [Grammar Check] 各種疑問文・It の特別用法

21

各種疑問文

1. 付加疑問文（be 動詞・助動詞）

1) Tom is a tall boy**, isn't he**?

2) Nancy isn't his sister**, is she**?

3) Kazuo can swim fast**, can't he**?

4) This is a good ball-point pen**, isn't it**?

5) There is a big hotel on the hill**, isn't there**? （主語は a big hotel）

2. 付加疑問文（一般動詞）

6) Keiko likes playing tennis very much**, doesn't she**?

7) Ben doesn't like sweet peppers**, does he**?

8) Ken and Akiko went on a picnic yesterday**, didn't they**?

9) He walks very fast**, doesn't he**? Yes, he does. / No, he doesn't.

10) Be quiet**, will you**? / Let's go there**, shall we**?

3. 間接疑問文

11) I know **who he is**.

12) I don't know **why you called me**.

13) Can you guess **when Tom will come**?

It の特別用法

1. 天候・距離・明暗などを表す it

14) **It** is fine today.

15) **It** is about two miles from this park to my house.

16) **It** gets dark here before five in winter.

2. 時刻・月日・季節などを表す it

17) **It** is summer here in Japan now.

18) What day of the month is **it** today? **It** is November 3.

19) What time is **it** by your watch? **It** is eight o'clock.

3. 形式主語・目的語の it

20)-1 **It** is fun **to** swim in the sea.

20)-2 **It** is easy **for** you **to** answer the question.

21) I found **it** important **to** study English every day.

Exercises

A. 付加疑問文をつけて英文を完成させなさい.

1. Mike and Tom love little animals, ____________?
2. Your father drove the car, ____________?
3. Tom was swimming in the pool, ____________?
4. Mother didn't play the violin, ____________?
5. There are some boys in the playground, ____________?

B. (　) 内の語句を正しく並べ替えなさい.

1. (what / you / Yuki / do / know / wants)?

   ……………………………………………………………………

2. We don't (didn't / you / why / to school / know / come) yesterday.

   ……………………………………………………………………

3. (do / lives / think / where / you / he)?

   ……………………………………………………………………

4. (came / tell / can / he / you / me / how / here)?

   ……………………………………………………………………

C. 次の英文を日本文に直しなさい.

1. It is a quarter to ten. ……………………………………………
2. It is two kilometers from here to the station.

   ……………………………………………………………………

3. It was very windy yesterday. ……………………………………………
4. It is quite natural for her to say so. ……………………………………………
5. It is getting colder tonight. ……………………………………………

D. 下線部に適語を入れて日本文に合う英文を完成させなさい.

1. ここから駅まで距離にしてどのくらいありますか.

   ………… far is ………… from here to the station?

2. １０時半です.

   ………… ………… ten thirty. = ………… ………… ………… past ………… .

3. 歴史の本を読むのはとてもおもしろい.

   ………… is very ………… ………… read a history book.

4. 梅雨にはたくさん雨が降ります.

   ………… rains a lot in the rainy season.

5. その問題を解くのは彼女にとって難しい.

   ………… is difficult ………… her ………… solve the problem.

Rearranging ▶▶▶ (　) 内の語に 1 語加えて並べ替え，和文に合う英文にしなさい．

1. 君はどうやって通学しているの．電車で．　(go / school / do / to / you)?　By train.

2. 彼女はカナダ人ですか，それともアメリカ人ですか．
(a / an / she / American / Canadian / is)?

3. 君の兄さんはスキーができますよね．　(can / brother / ski, / he / your)?

4. アリスはコーヒーが好きではありませんね．　(doesn't / she / like / coffee, / Alice)?

5. 誰がそこに住んでいるか知っていますか．　(you / lives / know / there / do)?

6. 君は彼がどこに住んでいると思いますか．　(think / lives / you / he / do)?

7. 招待して下さって有り難うございます．　(is / of / to / me / very / you / kind / invite).

8. 彼がそこにいたのは明らかだ．　(is / that / was / evident / he / there).

9. 悪いのは Tom です．　(blame / that / is / is / Tom / to).

Basic Composition ▶▶▶ 文末の (　) 内の条件をヒント（動詞は原形で提示）に英訳しなさい．

1. 言葉の力を理解することは大切だと思う．　(it, speech を含んで 10 語で)

2. 来たい人は誰でも歓迎されるでしょう．　(whoever, welcome を含んで 7 語で)

3. どちらへ行ったらいいのかわからない．　(don't, way を含んで 8 語で)

4. 来たい時はいつでもおいでなさい．　(can, to を含んで 7 語で)

5. テニスをしましょうよ．　(付加疑問を含んで 5 語で)

6. ペンをどこに置いたかな．　(wonder および現在完了形を含んで 8 語で)

7. ぜひ我が家にお越し下さい．　(why を含む 7 語からなる疑問文で)

8. 君はどのようにして英単語を覚えていますか．　(learn を含んで 6 語で)

Rewriting ▶▶▶ 次の各組の文がほぼ同じ意味になるように，（　）内に適語を書き入れなさい．

1. I'm disappointed at your report card. = Your report card is (　　　　　　).
2. It is easy to find her house. = You cannot (　　　　　　) her house.
3. He answered in the affirmative. = He said, "(　　　　　　)."
4. To my surprise, he died suddenly. = His sudden (　　　　　　) surprised me.
5. The fund-raiser scraped up quite a little money.
   = The fund-raiser scraped up (　　　　　　) money.
6. Be careful when you cross the street. = Be careful (　　　　　　) crossing the street.
7. He is not as strong as his brother. = He is (　　　　　　) strong than his brother.
8. No matter what she says, I won't believe her.
   = (　　　　　　) she says, I won't believe her.
9. We hope to see you again soon. = We hope we (　　　　　　) see you again soon.
10. He gave me some of the apples. = He didn't give me (　　　　　　) of the apples.

▶▶▶ Road to Science & Tech English (A10) ▶▶▶

Put into English ▶▶▶ 語句を並べ替えて，日本文に合う英文にしなさい．

1. 穴の開いた板は狭い台所では非常に便利である．柄のあるものはほとんどなんでも，多種多様の大きさや形の留め金を使って吊るすことができる．板は壁から5ミリほど離して付けねばならない．

   (is greatly convenient / pegboard / in a small kitchen / a perforated). (on it from hooks / almost anything / can be hung / of many shapes and sizes / with a handle). (must be spaced / from the wall / remember that / about 5 mm away / the board).

   ....

   ....

2. 金属がピカピカするのは，光を吸収したり通したりしないで，むしろ反射するからである．

   (are shiny; / metals / light rather / or transmit it / they reflect / than absorb it).

   ....

3. 電算機の速度と性能が向上するにつれて，プログラムも必然的に複雑になる．

   (in speed / as computers / and efficiency, / increase / the sophistication / they can handle / increase in / there is / of their programs / an inevitable)

   ....

   ....

Some Problems in Dam-Building

22

(ダム建設の問題点)

Engineers try to build dams that will stand a long time. Every man who has ever worked on a dam hopes that it will endure as long as the wonderful structures built in ancient Egypt. But sometimes the constant pressure of the water on a dam makes it break. In ancient times, the water often broke through the dam because the people neglected it.

Today dams are better built and they are not neglected. Most of them are as strong as anything in the world can possibly be. But even these dams sometimes break, and bring tragedy to the people living downstream of the dams.

In 1959 this happened in Spain and France. The dam in Spain was only two years old. The huge reservoir was still filling. During the winter the rain was very heavy. Then, on the night of January 9, 1959, the reservoir reached its full height. More water came pouring in. The water went over the top of the dam. Under this strain, the dam broke. The broken dam in France was also caused by heavy rain. A 200-ft-high dam which had been built in 1954 broke in December, 1959. A solid wall of water swept down on a vacation town. Engineers later discovered that the foundation rock had shifted along a thin line of clay. This weakened the dam and the extra weight of heavy rains made it break. We learn from our mistakes. When the dam in France broke, other dams similar to it were being built in Europe. These dams were redesigned to be much stronger.

Words & Phrases: **that will stand (for) a long time** 長持ちするだろう（ところの） **hopes** の主語は **Every man** **it will endure** = the dam will stand（持ちこたえる）a long time **as long as the wonderful structures ~** ～（に建てられた）素晴らしい建築物のように長い間 **built** = which were built **constant pressure of the water on a dam** 水がダムに間断なく与える圧力 **makes it break** ダムを破壊する **broke through the dam** ダムを突破した **neglected it** ダムの管理や手入れを怠る (neglect = give too little attention or care) **as strong as anything in the world can possibly be** この世で一番堅固な **bring tragedy to the people** 人々へ悲劇をもたらす **living downstream of the dams** ダムの下流に住んでいる **reservoir** 貯水池 **was still filling** まだ（水で）いっぱいになっていた **the rain was very heavy** 大雨が降った **reached its full height** 最上部に達した **under this strain** この重い負担で **solid wall** しっかりした厚い壁 (solid = firm; thick) **a vacation town** 保養地 **foundation rock** 基礎の岩石 **had shifted along a thin line of clay** 薄い層の粘土にそって移動していた **similar to ~** = which were similar to ~

Vocabulary

語頭文字と文字数をヒントに綴りなさい.

01. 壊す　b-(5字)	02. 耐える　e-(6)	03. 古代の　a-(7)	04. 持ちこたえる　s-(5)
05. 怠る　n-(7)	06. 悲劇　t-(7)	07. 下流に　d-(10)	08. 巨大な　h-(4)
09. 貯水池　r-(9)	10. 1月　J-(7)	11. 高さ　h-(6)	12. 注ぐ　p-(4)
13. 重い負担　s-(6)	14. 12月　D-(8)	15. どっと流れる　s-(5)	16. わかる　d-(8)
17. 基礎　f-(10)	18. 移動する　s-(5)	19. 粘土　c-(4)	20. 弱める　w-(6)
21. 余分な　e-(5)	22. 重さ　w-(6)	23. 過ち　m-(7)	24. 再設計する　r-(8)

Q & A

1) What kinds of dam do engineers try to build?

2) What sometimes makes a dam break?

3) Why did the water often break through the dam in ancient times?

4) What happened in Spain and France in 1959?

5) How high was the dam which broke in December, 1959?

Chapter 11-2 [Grammar Check] 受動態

1. S ＋ V ＋ O の文

23

1) Everybody **respects** Tom. → Tom **is respected by** everybody.

2) He **washed** the car. → The car **was washed by** him.

3) They **speak** English in America. → English **is spoken (by them)** in America.

2. S ＋ V ＋ O ＋ O の文

4) She **teaches us** English. → We **are taught English by** her.
→ English **is taught to us by** her.

5) He **bought her** a doll. → A doll **was bought for her by** him.
※ 動詞が buy や make などの場合は，ふつう間接目的語を主語にした受動態にはしない．

6) I **asked him** a trivial question. → He **was asked** a trivial question **by** me.
→ A trivial question **was asked of him by** me.

3. S ＋ V ＋ O ＋ C の文

7) They **elected** him **mayor**. → He **was elected mayor** (by them).

8) I found the book interesting. → The book **was found interesting by** me.

9) We call the dog "**Shiro.**" → The dog **is called** "**Shiro**" (by us).
※ 補語 (C) は，受動態の主語にはなれない．

4. by 以外の前置詞を使う受動態

10) Everybody here **knows** him. → He **is known to** everybody here.

11) The sight **surprised** her. → She **was surprised at** the sight.

12) The news **pleased** us. → We **were pleased with** the news.
※驚く，喜ぶなどの感情を表す場合，英語では受動態を用いるが，日本語では「～される」と訳さない方がより自然である .

5. 助動詞のある文

13) I **must do** the work today. → The work **must be done** (by me) today.

14) We **can see** that mountain. → That mountain **can be seen** (by us).

15) You **should study** English harder. → English **should be studied** harder (by you).

6. 受動態と否定文と疑問文

16) They **don't sell** books at the store. → Books **aren't sold** at the store.

17) **Do** they **sell** books at the store? → **Are** books **sold** at the store?

18) She **didn't invite** me to the party. → I **wasn't invited** to the party by her.

19) **Did** she **invite** him to the party? → **Was** he **invited** to the party by her?

20) **Nobody thanked** me. → I **was not thanked by anybody**.

Exercises

A. 次の英文を受動態に書き替えなさい.

1. Everybody loves his mother.
2. She read the book.
3. He taught them Chinese.
4. She cooked me some sausages.
5. We painted the door green.

B. 次の英文の（　）内から適当な語句を選びなさい.

1. I was driven to school by (he, his, him).
2. She is (pleased, pleasing, to please) with her new dress.
3. The tree was (cut, cutting, cuts) down by John.
4. (Did, Was, Had) the top of the mountain covered with snow?
5. (Are you interested, Are you interest, Do you interest) in world history?

C. 次の英文の（　）内から適語を選びなさい.

1. Butter is made (by, into, from) milk.
2. The chair is made (of, by, from) wood.
3. Milk is made (of, into, by) cheese.
4. The desks are made (into, from, by) them.
5. The car is made (at, in, by) Japan.

D. 次の日本文を ( ) 内の語句を使って受動態の英文に直しなさい.

1. この犬小屋は彼が作りました.　(doghouse)
2. この古い車は今は使われていません.　(old car)
3. この歌は若い人たちによく歌われています.　(often, young)
4. 彼女はそのプレゼントに満足しています.　(satisfied)
5. そのバケツ (bucket) には水がいっぱい入っています.　(filled)

Rearranging ▶▶▶ （　）内の語に 1 語加えて並べ替え，和文に合う英文にしなさい．

1. 彼女は私に毎日 3 度の食事を作ってくれる．
(cooked / a day / are / for / meals / me / by / three).

2. あの机は誰によってこわされましたか． (by / broken / that / was / desk)?

3. この辺りの店は 7 時に閉められます． (here / around / at / the / seven / are / stores).

4. 彼が楽しそうに歌うのが聞こえました． (merrily / heard / he / to / was).

5. 昨日，外国人に話しかけられた． (I / yesterday / spoken / foreigner / by / was / a).

6. その店は 9 時に開き，18 時まで開いています．
(the store / is / is / at / open / opened / 9 / 18 / , and).

7. 真相が多くの人にわかってきた． (the / many / got / truth / people / known).

8. 彼の同僚たちは彼のことをよく言う． (he / his / of / by / spoken / colleagues / is).

9. 彼の家が今建築中です． (his / now / being / house / built).

Basic Composition ▶▶▶ 文末の（　）内の条件をヒント（動詞は原形で提示）に英訳しなさい．

1. アメリカはコロンブスによって発見されました． (5 語で)

2. 私は Taro からこの本をもらいました． (given を含んで 7 語で)

3. 私たちはその犬に Shun と名づけた． (named を含んで 7 語で)

4. この小説は Hemingway の作ではない． (novel, was を含んで 7 語で)

5. カナダでは英語とフランス語が話されています． (are, in を含んで 7 語で)

6. 来週は会合が開かれます． (will, held を含んで 7 語で)

7. その猫は彼女に世話されるでしょう． (be, care を含んで 9 語で)

8. そのケーキはすでに彼女に食べられてしまった． (has, her を含んで 8 語で)

Rewriting ▶▶▶ 次の各組の文がほぼ同じ意味になるように，(　) 内に適語を書き入れなさい.

1. It's better for you to stay at home. = You (　　　　　) better stay at home.
2. They are building a bridge. = A bridge is (　　　　　) built by them.
3. She was so lucky that she got a job. = She was lucky (　　　　　) to get a job.
4. It is time for you to leave here. = It is time you (　　　　　) here.
5. This is a picture he took last year. = This is a picture (　　　　　) by him last year.
6. I have never been to Hawaii before. = This is my (　　　　　) visit to Hawaii.
7. There is nothing more precious than time. = Nothing is so precious (　　　　　) time.
8. If only she helped me. = I (　　　　　) she helped me.
9. He said to me, "Where is your school?" = He (　　　　　) me where my school was.
10. He stood up so that he might greet her. = He stood up in (　　　　　) to greet her.

▶▶▶ Road to Science & Tech English (A11) ▶▶▶

Put into English ▶▶▶ 語句を並べ替えて，日本文に合う英文にしなさい.

1. バッテリーが電流を送っているか否かをテストするには，ヘッドライトかフロントガラスのワイパーのスイッチを入れてみることである．バッテリーは通常エンジンの側か，モデルによっては，後部荷物入れか後部座席の下についている．
(on the headlights / to test / switch / or the windshield wipers / is supplying current / if the battery). The battery (although / beside the engine, / in the trunk / is usually / or under / it is / in some models) the backseat.

2. 水道主管は氷結害を避けるために，一般に地下 90 センチ以上の深さに埋設させる.
(about 3 feet / below the ground surface / are generally / or more / water mains / laid / them / frost damage / to protect / from).

3. ガラスは電子に対して不透明 (電子を通さないの意) であるから，電子を集めるのにガラスのレンズを使うことはできない.
(opaque to / since / electrons, / glass is / to focus / glass lenses / them / cannot be used).

Concrete Construction
(コンクリート建築)

24

The three basic symptoms of distress in concrete are cracking, spalling, and disintegration of the surface. Spalling and disintegration are readily detected as major cracks. Fine cracks are not.

To locate fine cracks, inspect the concrete surface closely. Also, look for efflorescence, that is, coatings or drippings of white lime, often in the form of stalactites. Efflorescence is a sign that water is leaking through the concrete, dissolving some of the lime, and depositing it on the downstream face of the concrete as the water evaporates. Efflorescence is usually a sign of the presence of a crack, although it is sometimes due merely to porous concrete. In either case, a defect or a defective area is present.

Cracks which are normally invisible will show up on a wet surface that is just drying. If it is feasible, wet the concrete surface in question thoroughly and return to inspect it later. As the surface dries, the cracks will retain moisture and show up as dark lines on the background.

Any sign of dampness, especially ponded or running water, on the concrete surface, is a sign of trouble or incipient trouble and should be investigated.

Corrosion of reinforcing bars normally is accompanied by rust staining of the adjacent concrete surface. Rust stains are easily detected, and should be noted. When rust staining is found, chip out the concrete locally to uncover the bar and check its condition.

Words & Phrases: **symptoms of distress** 悩みの徴候　**cracking** ひび割れ　**spalling** 裂けること　**disintegration** 崩壊；風化　**fine** 細かい　**locate** 突き止める　**efflorescence** 擬花；白華（石材やコンクリートなどの表面にできる白い結晶）**coatings** 被覆；コーティング　**drippings** しずく　**lime** 石灰　**dissolving ~, and depositing ~** ～を融解させ，溶着させる　**on the downstream face of ~** ～の流れに沿った表面に　**it is sometimes due merely to ~** たんに～に起因することが時々ある（が）　**porous** 多孔性の　**a defect or a defective area** 欠陥，つまり，欠陥部　**invisible** = which are invisible　**show up** 現れる　**feasible** = possible　**retain moisture** 水分が逃げないように保つ　**the background** 地（じ）　**dampness** 湿気　**ponded or running water** 水がたまっていても流れていても　**incipient trouble** 初期のトラブル　**corrosion of reinforcing bars** 鉄筋の腐食　**is accompanied by ~** ～に随伴して起こる　**rust staining** さびのよごれ　**the adjacent concrete surface** 隣接するコンクリートの表面　**rust stains** さびによるよごれ箇所　**chip out ~ locally** ～を局部的にけずる　**to uncover the bar** 鉄筋を露出させる

Vocabulary

語頭文字と文字数をヒントに綴りなさい.

01. 徴候 s-(7字)	02. 悩み d-(8)	03. ひび割れ c-(8)	04. 裂けること s-(8)
05. 崩壊 d-(14)	06. すぐに r-(7)	07. 見つける d-(6)	08. 細かい f-(4)
09. 突き止める l-(6)	10. 擬花 e-(13)	11. 被覆 c-(7)	12. しずく d-(8)
13. 石灰 l-(4)	14. 鍾乳石 s-(10)	15. もれる l-(4)	16. 溶かす d-(8)
17. 溶着する d-(7)	18. 蒸発する e-(9)	19. 多孔性の p-(6)	20. 目に見えない i-(9)
21. 実行可能な f-(8)	22. 初期の i-(9)	23. 補強する r-(9)	24. 暴露する u-(7)

Q & A

1) Which of the three basic symptoms of distress in concrete isn't readily detected as major cracks?

2) What are coatings or drippings of white lime called?

3) What kind of sign is efflorescence?

4) How will the cracks show up as the surface dries?

5) Why should the concrete be chipped out locally?

Chapter 12-2 [Grammar Check] 完了形

1. 現在完了 ＜ have (has) + 過去分詞 ＞ (継続・完了・結果・経験)
過去の動作・状態が現在と何らかのつながりを持っていることを示す. 25

1) Bill **has been** in Japan since last year.

2) I **haven't seen** him since Monday.

3) I **have known** her for five years.
cf. 過去のある時に始まった**動作**が現在まで**継続**している場合は，現在完了進行形を用いる.
They **have been playing** baseball for two hours. （2 時間ずっとしている）

4) I **have already washed** the dishes.

5) **Have** you **done** your homework **yet**? No, **not yet**.

6) Spring **has come**.

7) I **have visited** Paris five times.

8) **Have** you ever **been** to Mexico?

9) He **has** never **climbed** Mt. Fuji.
＊現在完了は，常に現在に視点を置いているので，**過去を示すような語句**と共に用ない.
(×) He has climbed Mt. Fuji **last year**. (×) **When** have you been to Italy?

2. 過去完了 ＜ had + 過去分詞 ＞
過去のある時までの完了 (結果)・経験・継続を表す. それぞれの用法は現在完了に準じる.

10) The train **had** already **started** when I arrived at the station. （完了）

11) I **had** never **met** him before that. （経験）

12) We **had lived** in Kyoto until then. （継続）

13) I lost the pen that I **had bought** the day before. （大過去）

3. 未来完了 ＜ will [shall] + have + 過去分詞 ＞
未来のある時までの完了 (結果)・経験・継続を表す. それぞれの用法は現在完了に準じる.

14) He **will have finished** studying by five. （完了）

15) If I go to Hawaii again, I **will have visited** it ten times. （経験）

16) They **will have been** here for six years by next May. （継続）

Exercises

A. 次の英文の（　）内から適当な語句を選びなさい.

1. I (don't, didn't, haven't) seen Tom since last week.
2. Ann (loses, lost, has lost) her bag three days ago.
3. I have (knew, known, knowing) Janet for ten years.
4. Mother (goes, gone, has gone) shopping. She isn't at home now.
5. They (sell, have sold, will have sold) all the furniture by next month.
6. I knew her at once, for I (saw, have seen, had seen) her before.

B. 次の日本文に合うように(　　)に適語を入れなさい.

1. 今まで京都を訪れたことがありますか. Have you (　　　　) (　　　　) Kyoto?
2. 朝食をちょうど食べたところです. I have (　　　　) (　　　　) breakfast.
3. 吉雄はもう出発しましたか. Has Yoshio left (　　　　)?
4. どのくらいの間ここにいるのですか. (　　　　) (　　　　) have you been here?
5. 今まで一度も北海道に行ったことがありません. I have (　　) (　　) to Hokkaido.
6. 彼女はフランスに行く前にフランス語を勉強したことがなかった.
   She (　　　　) (　　　　) (　　　　) French before she went to France.
7. もし彼がもう一度霧島に行くと，そこに１０回行ったことになります.
   If he visits Kirishima again, he (　　　　) (　　　　) (　　　　) it ten times.

C. 各質問文に対して，適切な応答文を右から選びなさい.

1. Have you read the book yet? (　　)　a) For three years.
2. How long have you been in Japan? (　　)　b) Yes, I have. Twice.
3. Have you ever climbed the mountain? (　　)　c) No, not yet.
4. When did you come home? (　　)　d) Just an hour ago.

D. 各文の下線部の誤りを正しなさい.

1. She showed him the pictures she painted in Paris.
2. My father died after he is sick for a long time.
3. Next July we have married for fifty years.
4. I read the novel through by tomorrow.

Rearranging ▶▶▶ (　) 内の語に1語加えて並べ替え，和文に合う英文にしなさい．

1. この辺りの木の葉はすっかり落ちてしまいました．
(here / all / leaves / have / around / the).

2. Tom は London を発って Edinburgh に向かいました．
(has / London / Edinburgh / Tom / left).

3. 父が亡くなって 10 年になる．　(dead / years / father / ten / been / my / has).

4. 私は生まれたときからここに住んでいます．(here / I / I / lived / was / have / born).

5. どこへ行ってきたのですか？ 公園へ行ってきたところです．
(you / have / where)? (to / the / have / I / park).

6. 君は以前佐賀にいたことがありますか．　(been / Saga / have / before / you)?

7. 私はその前日買ったペンを無くしてしまいました．
(which / I / I / the / before / bought / lost / pen / the day).

8. 彼らはちょうど今戻ってきたところです．(come / just / they / back).

9. 正午までにそれを終えてしまっているでしょう．(I / by / it / will / noon / finished).

Basic Composition ▶▶▶ 文末の (　) 内の条件をヒント (動詞は原形で提示) に英訳しなさい．

1. 新薬に関する報告書を書いたところです．　(I, just, on を含んで 10 語で)

2. 彼らはまだそこに到着していない．　(not, yet を含んで 6 語で)

3. 彼女は先月から福岡に滞在しています．　(stayed を含んで 8 語で)

4. すぐに彼女だとわかった，というのは以前に話しかけたことがあったから．
(recognized, at, to を含んで 12 語で)

5. 会合は私がそこに着いた時には始まっていた．　(had, there を含んで 8 語で)

6. 私は彼女と知り合って 5 年で結婚した．　(had, for, when, we を含んで 10 語で)

7. 私がこの本を再度読めば，三度読んだことになる．　(I, if, it を含んで 13 語で)

Rewriting ▶▶▶ 次の各組の文がほぼ同じ意味になるように，(　) 内に適語を書き入れなさい.

1. You don't have to worry about it. = You (　　　　　　) not worry about it.
2. A foreigner spoke to me. = I was (　　　　　　) to by a foreigner.
3. She lived till she was a hundred. = She lived to (　　　　　　) a hundred.
4. The dream cannot be realized easily. = The dream cannot come (　　　　　　) easily.
5. He is good at playing tennis. = He is a good tennis (　　　　　　).
6. You must not play here. = (　　　　　　) play here.
7. He is responsible for the accident. = He is to (　　　　　　) for the accident.
8. She cries like a baby. = She cries (　　　　　　) if she were a baby.
9. He suggested that they should play after school.
   = He said, "(　　　　　　) play after school."
10. He became a good scholar by diligence. = Diligence (　　　　　　) him a good scholar.

▶▶▶ Road to Science & Tech English (A12) ▶▶▶

Put into English ▶▶▶ 語句を並べ替えて，日本文に合う英文にしなさい.

1. 金属は，対重量強度比率は高いし，固くて耐久力があり，複雑な形につくりあげることができる.
   (strength-to-weight / have / ratio / metals / a high). (hard / they / and durable / are). (formed / complex shapes / can be / they / into).

2. 人工衛星が送信してきたデータから，船に搭載したコンピュータが，送信の初めと終りに，衛星の位置を計算して求める.
   (data, / the satellite-transmitted / from / calculates / of the satellite / a ship-borne computer / the position / and end / at the beginning / of the transmission).

3. 自動防止装置が組み込まれているため，油圧装置が作動するので，台が行き過ぎることなく事故を未然に防いでいます.
   (prohibits an / by means of / the automatic governor / overrun of / the oil pressure system, / the table / will prevent / which / accidents).

A Dangerous Gas

（危険なガス）

26

One of the dangerous gaseous air pollutants is carbon monoxide. Only one part per 100,000 will cause illness, but one part per 750 will cause death in 30 minutes. This gas, a mixture of carbon and oxygen, is most often associated with the exhaust gas that comes from automobiles. Actually, carbon monoxide is not usually a serious pollutant in our air. In large amounts it is certainly poisonous. But most of the time the amount of carbon monoxide in the air is not great enough to cause any damage to human health.

For every 1,000 gallons of gasoline burned in automobile engines, about 3,000 pounds of carbon monoxide enter the air. Even considering this large amount of gas, research scientists have said for years that carbon monoxide was not a dangerous gas when given off into the open air.

Recently, however, more scientific evidence is being found that should make us more doubtful of carbon monoxide—even in the open air. It is known that carbon monoxide reduces the ability of the blood to carry oxygen. This means that there will be an added strain on the heart as more blood must be carried much more rapidly through the body. Also strain is put on the breathing system as it must bring more and more oxygen into the lungs. Some scientists think that many of the automobile accidents that have been blamed on tiredness were probably caused by slight cases of carbon monoxide poisoning.

Words & Phrases: **gaseous** 気体の　**air pollutant** 大気汚染物質 cf. air pollution 大気汚染　**carbon monoxide** 一酸化炭素　**one part per 100,000** 10万分率 cf. ppm = parts per million 100万分率　**will** 習性・特性・傾向などを表す **750** = 750 parts　**mixture** 化合物　**oxygen** 酸素　**is associated with ~** ~を連想させる　**exhaust gas** 排気ガス　**poisonous** 有毒な　**most of the time** 殆んどの場合　**is not great enough to cause any damage to ~** （健康を）害するほどひどくない　**gallon** ガロン（液量の単位．米国の標準ガロン = 3.785 ℓ，英国の標準ガロン = 4.546 ℓ．）　**burned** = which is burned　**research scientist** 科学研究者　**when given off into the open air** = when it was given off into the open air 一酸化炭素が大気中へ放出されれば　**more scientific evidence** 更に多くの科学的なデータ　**that should make us more doubtful of ~** ～を一層疑わしくさせる（と思われる）ところの　**reduces the ability of the blood to carry oxygen** 血液が酸素を運ぶ能力を減退させる　**there will be an added strain on ~** ～に（極度の）緊張が加わるだろう　**breathing system** 呼吸器系統　**that have been blamed on tiredness** 疲れのせいにされてきているところの　**slight cases of carbon monoxide poisoning** 一酸化炭素中毒の軽い症状

Vocabulary

語頭文字と文字数をヒントに綴りなさい.

01. 危険な d-(9字)	02. 気体の g-(7)	03. 汚染物質 p-(9)	04. 炭素 c-(6)
05. 一酸化物 m-(8)	06. 化合物 m-(7)	07. 連想する a-(9)	08. 排気 e-(7)
09. 危ない s-(7)	10. 毒素 p-(9)	11. 酸素 o-(6)	12. 証拠；事実 e-(8)
13. 疑わしい d-(8)	14. 減じる r-(6)	15. 能力 a-(7)	16. 緊張 s-(6)
17. 速く r-(7)	18. 呼吸する b-(7)	19. 肺 l-(4)	20. 責める b-(5)
21. 疲れ t-(9)	22. 引き起こす c-(5)	23. 軽い s-(6)	24. 中毒 p-(9)

Q & A

1) How much carbon monoxide will cause death in 30 minutes?

2) What kind of mixture is carbon monoxide?

3) What happens when 1,000 gallons of gasoline are burned in automobile engines?

4) In the opinion of research scientists, wasn't cabon monoxide a dangerous gas when given off into the open air?

5) What does carbon monoxide reduce?

Chapter 13-2 [Grammar Check] 接続詞 II（時制の一致を含む）

27

1. 等位接続詞 (See Ch. 5)

1) It is late, **so** you had better go home soon.
2) It may rain soon, **for** it is getting cloudy.

2.「時」,「条件」を表す従属接続詞 (See Ch. 5)

3) **As soon as** he came home, his mother went out.
4) I usually jog a few miles **before** I have breakfast.
5) You must not come in **unless** I tell you to.

3.「譲歩」,「原因・理由」などを表す従属接続詞 (See Ch. 5)

6) **Though** she is very tired, she has something to do tonight.
7) **Since** I didn't know the answer, I kept silent.
8) I'm glad **that** he won first prize at the exhibition.

4. 名詞節を導く従属接続詞

9) It is certain **that** Dick was there at that time.
10) The news **that** he is alive makes us happy.
11) The fact is **that** I don't like vegetables.
12) I don't know **whether** he will go to Britain (**or not**).

5. その他の従属接続詞

13) He is **so** tall **that** he can touch the ceiling.
14) Get up **as** early **as you can**.
15) Do **as** you like.
16) I am taller **than** Alice is.

6. 時制の一致

17) She **says** that she **is** happy. → She **said** that she **was** happy.
18) I **believe** that they **are** honest. → I **believed** that they **were** honest.
19) I **think** that she **was** ill. → I **thought** that she **had been** ill.
20) It **seems** that he **sold** the house. → It **seemed** that he **had sold** the house.
※ 時制の一致の例外（不変の真理，現在の習慣など）
21) The teacher **says** that the earth **moves** around the sun. （不変の真理)
→ The teacher **said** that the earth **moves** around the sun.
22) She **says** that she **goes** to bed at ten every night. （現在の習慣）
→ She **said** that she **goes** to bed at ten every night.
23) He **teaches** us that Columbus **discovered** America. （歴史上の事実）
→ He **taught** us that Columbus **discovered** America.
24) I **wish** I **had** a yacht.（仮定法）→ I **wished** I **had** a yacht.

Exercises

A. (　) 内に入る適語を下の語群から選び，書き入れなさい.

1. She was poor, (　　　　　) she was happy.
2. Let's go home (　　　　　) it gets dark.
3. It is morning, (　　　　　) the cocks are crowing.
4. I am sorry (　　　　　) I cannot help you.

[but / though / before / for / that]

B. 次の各組の文が同じ意味になるように (　) 内に適語を入れなさい.

1. He is very old, but he works hard. = (　　　　　) he is very old, he works hard.
2. Run, and you'll catch the bus. = (　　　　　) you run, you'll catch the bus.
3. She was so busy that she couldn't attend the meeting.
   = She was (　　　　　) busy (　　　　　) attend the meeting.

C. 次の日本文を ( ) 内に与えられた語句を使って英文に直しなさい.

1. 彼はその前の週から病気だったようだ.　(seemed, been, previous)
2. できるだけ早くここへ来てください.　(soon, can)
3. 遅い時間ですが , 私たちはもう少しいます.　(though, a little)
4. 彼は病気ではないかと心配です.　(afraid, may)

D. 次の各文の下線部を過去時制にして全文を書き替えなさい.

1. He doesn't know that the Civil War broke out in 1861.
2. She thinks that the sun moves round the earth.

E. 次の英文の誤りを訂正しなさい.

1. The boy didn't know that Cuba was an island country.
2. My little daughter answered that four and three were seven.
3. The other day he told me that he has seen me by the lake three years ago.
4. The teacher asked me why was I late for school.

Rearranging ▶▶▶ （　）内の語に1語加えて並べ替え，和文に合う英文にしなさい.

1. 暗くなったので，私は家路を急いだ.　(home / it / we / dark, / so / got).

2. 昨日私は家にいました，というのは雪が降ったからです.
(yesterday, / I / it / stayed / was / home / snowing / at).

3. 彼に今日は暇かどうか尋ねなさい.　(free / ask / is / today / he / him).

4. 雨が止むまでここで待ちましょうか.　(wait / rain / shall / stops / here / we / the)?

5. 天候不良のため試合は中止になった.
(the / the / called / bad / was / was / weather / off / game).

6. 子供の頃は貧しかったが幸せでした. (I / I / was / was / though / poor / in / my / happy).

7. 第二次世界大戦は1945年に終わったと習いました.
(1945 / learned / we / in / World / II / War / that).

Basic Composition ▶▶▶ 文末の（　）内の条件をヒント（動詞は原形で提示）に英訳しなさい.

1. 私は彼が忙しいと思った.　(that を含んで6語で)

2. Dick はそのホテルに泊まっていると言った.　(that を含んで9語で)

3. 彼らは地球は丸いと信じていた.　(that, round を含んで7語で)

4. マイクは彼女が買い物に行ってしまったと思った.　(that を含んで7語で)

5. Andrew は犯人ではないと思う.　(opinion, criminal を含んで9語で)

6. 彼女は知識だけでなく経験もある.　(has, not, but を含んで8語で)

7. 彼が来るかどうかは確かではない.　(whether, certain を含んで7語で)

8. 彼は時は金なりという信念に基づいて行動する.　(in, conviction を含んで9語で)

9. 鳥であればいいのになあ，と彼は言った.　(that, wished を含んで9語で)

Rewriting ▶▶▶ 次の各組の文がほぼ同じ意味になるように，(　) 内に適語を書き入れなさい．

1. I should have gone there. = I am sorry I (　　　　　) go there.
2. He earns a good income. = His salary is (　　　　　).
3. The key was not to be found. = The key (　　　　　) not be found.
4. Would you mind if I watch TV? = Would you mind my (　　　　　) TV?
5. Tom is busy. Ben is busy, too. = (　　　　　) Tom and Ben are busy.
6. Iraq intended to have invaded the country.
   = Iraq (　　　　　) intended to invade the country.
7. Not only he but also I am a student. = I as well as he (　　　　　) a student.
8. I'm sorry I am not twenty years younger.
   = I (　　　　　) I were twenty years younger.
9. He said, "The earth is round." = He said that the earth (　　　　　) round.
10. He is too honest to tell a lie. = His (　　　　　) won't allow him to tell a lie.

▶▶▶ Road to Science & Tech English (A13) ▶▶▶

Put into English ▶▶▶ 語句を並べ替えて，日本文に合う英文にしなさい．

1. 硝酸は沸点が80℃の無色で発煙性の液体である．化学式はHNO_3で，強力な酸化剤である．大抵の金属を侵蝕し，二酸化窒素の煙霧を出す．

   (80℃ / is / with / a colorless fuming liquid / nitric acid / the boiling point of). (the chemical formula / has / it / HNO_3). (oxidizing / nitric acid / a powerful / agent / is). (attacks / it / most metals, / fumes of / dioxide / producing / nitrogen).

2. アルコール燃料を使う理由は，アンチ・ノック性が高いのと，そのほかに，内部冷却作用という点で有利だからである．

   (from / its high / apart / antiknock value, / for using / one reason / alcohol fuel / its action / an internal / is / as) coolant.

3. ニューロンは刺激を受けると電気化学的パルスを発射する．そして，1度発射を終えると，その後約100分の1秒の間はパルスの発射はない．

   When (is / a neuron / stimulated, / emits / pulse, / it / an electrochemical / a period / there is / a hundredth / after which / of a second / of about / the neuron / emitted / during which / cannot be) again.

Urban Atmospheric Pollution

(都市の大気汚染)

28

Air pollution constitutes a serious problem and one that is becoming increasingly important with the increasing concentration of population in large urban centers. In one sense there is no way to discuss one part of air resources management without looking at the whole picture, but since the automobile is one of the principal offenders in Los Angeles and other California cities, and since California has established pollution control standards and is involved in a program of evaluating and approving control devices for motor vehicles, it may be well to point out what is going on there in the automotive field.

As the urban growth and suburban expansion of cities is planned and developed, rural and wild lands disappear. People in small communities will soon find themselves living in a large metropolis. With increased density of population the air use per unit area increases, and it becomes more and more difficult to maintain good air. The effect of accumulation of pollutants may become severe.

Urbanization brings questions of peripheral-pattern development. How are we to manage the stresses placed on all utilities—water supply, sewage disposal, storm drains, streets, highways, power systems, telephone, fire protection, and all materials of survival such as food and shelter? But overshadowing any of these in importance is the problem of air in sufficient quantity and quality for consumptive use by people and vegetation, and for combustion processes.

Words & Phrases: **atmospheric pollution** = air pollution 大気汚染　**constitutes** = makes up 構成する　**one** = a serious problem　**with the increasing concentration of ~** ～の集中化が激しくなるにつれて　**in one sense** = in a sense ある意味では　**there is no way to discuss ~** ～を議論することができない（次の without ... と呼応して「～を議論するには必ず…の必要がある」と考えるとよい）　**air resources management** 空気資源管理　**the whole picture** 全体の構想　**offenders** 犯罪者　**pollution control standards** 公害規制基準　**be involved in ~** ～に関与している　**evaluating** 調べる　**control devices** 制御装置　**motor vehicles** 自動車類　**it may be well to point out ~** ～を指摘するのが当然だろう　**there in the automotive field** その分野，つまり自動車産業分野に（there で大まかに位置を示し，in 以下で同格的に正確な位置を示している）　**suburban expansion** 郊外の拡大化　**a large metropolis** 大都市　**the air use per unit area** 単位面積当りの空気の使用量　**accumulation** 堆積　**pollutants** 汚染物　**peripheral-pattern development** 周辺機構の発展　**stresses** 圧迫；負担　**placed** = which are placed　**utilities** = public utilities 水道・ガス・電気など市民に対するサービスやその施設の総称　**sewage disposal** 下水処理　**storm drains** 大雨の排水路　**power systems** 発電系システム　**overshadowing ~ in importance is the problem ...** …の問題が～よりも重要になってきている　**combustion processes** 燃焼過程

Vocabulary

語頭文字と文字数をヒントに綴りなさい.

01. 都市の	u-(5字)	02. 大気の	a-(11)	03. 構成する	c-(10)	04. 集中	c-(13)
05. 資源	r-(9)	06. 管理	m-(10)	07. 主要な	p-(9)	08. 犯罪者	o-(8)
09. 制定する	e-(9)	10. 基準	s-(9)	11. 関係する	i-(8)	12. 評価する	e-(8)
13. 是認する	a-(7)	14. 乗り物	v-(7)	15. 自動車の	a-(10)	16. 郊外の	s-(8)
17. 密度	d-(7)	18. 堆積	a-(12)	19. 汚染物	p-(9)	20. 下水	s-(6)
21. 排水	d-(5)	22. 見劣りさせる	o-(10)	23. 消費の	c-(11)	24. 植物；植生	v-(10)

Q & A

1) What must we look at when we discuss one part of air resources management?

2) Why may it be well to point out what is going on there in the automotive field?

3) When do rural and wild lands disappear?

4) What becomes more and more difficult as population density increases?

5) What problem is the most important according to the last paragraph of the passage?

1. 仮定法過去 … 現在の事実に反対の仮定・想像を表す

29

If ＋ 主語 ＋ (助) 動詞の過去形 ; were / was} …, 主語 ＋ {would, should, could, might} ＋ 原形 ～

1) **If** I **knew** her telephone number, I **would** call her.
   = As I don't know her telephone number, I won't call her.

2) **If** my father **were** alive, he **could** see his grandson.
   = As my father is not alive, he cannot see his grandson.
   ∗ **Were I** a bird, I would fly to you soon.
   = **If I were** a bird, I would fly to you soon.

2. 仮定法過去完了 … 過去の事実に反対の仮定・想像を表す

If ＋ 主語 ＋ had ＋ 過去分詞} …, 主語 ＋ {would, should, could, might} ＋ have ＋ 過去分詞 ～

3) **If** he **had worked** hard, he **would have passed** the exam.
   = As he didn't work hard, he didn't pass the exam.

4) **If** it **had** not **been** snowing heavily, I **could have gone** out.
   = As it was snowing heavily, I couldn't go out.
   ∗ **Had he seen** you, he would have been happy.
   = **If he had seen** you, he would have been happy.

3. その他の仮定法

5) **If** it **should** rain on the way, we will turn back. 「万一…したら，～」
   < If ＋ 主語 ＋ should …, 主語 ＋ 助動詞 (過去形あるいは現在形) ～ . >

6) I **wish** (= **If only**) I **could** fly. = I am sorry I cannot fly.
   < I wish ＋ S ＋ 仮定法過去 ～ . >「～ であればよいのに」(現在の願望を表す)

7) I **wish** (= **If only**) I **had seen** the film. = I am sorry I didn't see the film.
   < I wish ＋ S ＋ 仮定法過去完了 ～ . >「～ であればよかったのに」(過去の願望を表す)

8) He speaks English **as if** he **were** a native speaker.「まるで ～ であるかのように」
   <主節 ＋ as if ＋ S ＋ 仮定法過去 ～ . >(主節の動詞の時と同時の事柄についての様態を表す)
   cf. He looks pale as if he had seen a ghost.

9) **It is time** you **went** to bed.
   < It is time ＋ S ＋ 仮定法過去 ～ . >「もう ～ すべき（してもよい）時間だ」

10) **If it were not for** you, we **could**n't carry out our plan. 「もし君がいなければ，～」
    = **But for** you, we **could**n't carry out our plan.
    = **Without** you, we **could**n't carry out our plan.
    cf. **If it had not been for** you, we **couldn't have carried out** our plan.

Exercises

A. 次の英文の（　）内から適当な語句を選びなさい.

1. He will help you if he (has, had, had had) time.
2. If my father (is, are, were) alive, I could go to college.
3. If I (have, had, had had) the money, I could have bought it.
4. If you did your best, you (could pass, had passed, could have passed) it.

B. 次の英文を仮定法を用いて書き替えなさい.

1. As the girl is weak, she can't walk all the way with us.

   ....

2. He is so old that he can't run so fast as you.

   ....

3. He did not study hard, so he failed in the examination.

   ....

4. As it was rainy yesterday, we could not go on a picnic.

   ....

C. 次の各組の文が同じ意味になるように（　）内に適語を入れなさい.

1. As I am not so young as you, I cannot play football.
   If I (　　　　) as young as you, I (　　　　) play football.
2. I could not write a longer letter because I didn't have more time.
   I could (　　　　) (　　　　) a longer letter if I (　　　　) had more time.
3. Should she change her mind, nobody would blame her.
   (　　　　) (　　　　) (　　　　) change her mind, nobody would blame her.
4. I am sorry I am not as beautiful as she.
   I (　　　　) (　　　　) (　　　　) as beautiful as she.
5. If he had seen you, he would have been happy.
   (　　　　) (　　　　) (　　　　) you, he would have been happy.

D. 次の日本文を（　）内の語句を使って英文に直しなさい.

1. 車があれば，あなたをドライブに連れて行ってあげるのですが.　(had, take)

   ....

2. 彼がもっと注意深ければ，同じ間違いはしないでしょう.　(careful, mistakes)

   ....

3. もし君が７時に家を出ていたら，７時半の電車に乗れたのに.　(the 7:30 train)

   ....

Rearranging ▶▶▶ (　) 内の語に１語加えて並べ替え，和文に合う英文にしなさい.

1. 彼はまるで酔っ払っているかのように話す.　(he / he / were / talks / drunk / as).

2. 私に姉がいたらなあ.　(only / a / had / I / sister)!

3. 車の運転を習っておけばよかったなあ.　(I / I / drive / learned / how / had / to).

4. 彼が話すのを聞けば，君は彼を韓国人と間違えるだろう.
(Korean / talk, / take / would / him / him / for / you / a / hear).

5. もし太陽がなければ, 何も生きられないだろう. (for / sun, / live / nothing / the / could).

6. もし彼の援助がなかったら，私は失敗しただろう.
(I / help, / had / his / would / failed / been / it / not / for).

7. せめて彼に侘びくらい言ってもいいだろう.　(apologize / you / least / him / to / at).

Basic Composition ▶▶▶ 文末の（　）内の条件をヒント（動詞は原形で提示）に英訳しなさい.

1. ギターを上手に弾くことができたらなあ.　(wish を含んで 8 語で)

2. もし車を持っていれば, 君をそこまで送っていくのですが.　(if, drive を含んで 10 語で)

3. その映画を見ておけばよかったなあと思った.　(wished を含んで 7 語で)

4. 万一明日雨が降れば, 私たちはピクニックに行きません.　(should rain を含んで 12 語で)

5. たとえ私が二百歳まで生きたとしても，その悲しい事故は決して忘れないだろう.
(were to live を含んで 18 語で)

6. もしあの時その土地を買っていたら，今頃は金持ちになっているはずです.
(then, should を含んで 12 語で)

7. 日本人なら別の行動をとっていただろう.　(differently を含んで 6 語で)

8. もし君が彼の立場ならどうしますか.　(what, place を含んで 7 語で)

9. その薬がなかったら，私は死んでしまったでしょう.　(but を含んで 8 語で)

Rewriting ▶▶▶ 次の各組の文がほぼ同じ意味になるように，（ ）内に適語を書き入れなさい．

1. It's natural for him to praise her. = He may ( ) praise her.
2. We must observe the traffic rules. = The traffic rules must ( ) observed.
3. I hope you will succeed. = I hope ( ) your success.
4. He insists that I should go there. = He insists ( ) my going there.
5. He directed us to the hotel. = He told us the ( ) to the hotel.
6. He speaks English better than I. = I don't speak English as ( ) as he.
7. This fact cannot be overstressed. = This fact cannot be stressed ( ) much.
8. Because of the wet road, the bus was late.

   = Thanks ( ) the wet road, the bus was late.
9. He said to me, "You are very kind." = He told me that ( ) was very kind.
10. He talks very little. = He is a man of few ( ).

▶▶▶ Road to Science & Tech English (A14) ▶▶▶

Put into English ▶▶▶ 語句を並べ替えて，日本文に合う英文にしなさい．

1. 電気毛布の機構は，比較的簡単であって，自由に曲がる発熱体で作られている．そして，これが 2 つの部分からなる材料の間に縫い込んである．

   An electric blanket (mainly of / is relatively / flexible heating / simple and / consists) elements. The elements (of material /are / between / sewn / two pieces).

   ....

   ....

2. 人間の宇宙旅行にとって無重力は極めて危険であると考えられたことがあった．しかし我々は宇宙飛行士がいともたやすく 1 カ月にわたって無重力状態に適応することを知っている．

   Weightlessness (manned space / was once / a serious / thought / to be / hazard to) travel; we know that (the astronaut / quite easily to / adapts themselves / it) up to a month.

   ....

   ....

Minerals in the Sea

（海中の鉱物）

30

The ocean is the earth's greatest storehouse of minerals. In a single cubic mile of sea water there are, on the average, 166 million tons of dissolved salts, and in all the ocean waters of the earth there are about 50 quadrillion tons. And it is in the nature of things for this quantity to be gradually increasing over the millennia, for although the earth is constantly shifting her component materials from place to place, the heaviest movements are forever seaward.

It has been assumed that the first seas were only faintly saline and that their saltiness has been growing over a long long period. For the primary source of the ocean's salt is the rocky mantle of the continents. When those first rains came—the centuries-long rains that fell from the heavy clouds enveloping the young earth—they began the processes of wearing away the rocks and carrying their contained minerals to the sea. The annual flow of water seaward is believed to be about 6,500 cubic miles, this inflow of river water adding to the ocean several billion tons of salts.

It is a curious fact that there is little similarity between the chemical composition of river water and that of sea water. The various elements are present in entirely different proportions. The rivers bring in four times as much calcium as chloride, for example, yet in the ocean the proportions are strongly reversed—46 times as much chloride as calcium.

Words & Phrases: **minerals** 鉱物　**cubic mile** 立方マイル　**on the average** 平均して　**dissolved salts** 溶解した塩（類）　**quadrillion** 1,000 兆（の）；英では 100 万の 4 乗　**over the millennia** 数千年に渡って sg. millennium　**is constantly shifting ~ from place to place** 地域により～を絶えず変えている　**component materials** 構成物質　**only faintly saline** ごく僅かな塩類（しか含んでいなかった）　**saltiness** 塩分　**the rocky mantle** 土岩層（表面が岩石に覆われた層）　**the centuries-long rains** = long rains over centuries　**the heavy clouds** 厚い雲　**enveloping** 直前の the heavy clouds にかかる　**of wearing away ~** ～を摩滅させることの　**carrying** the processes of に続く　**their contained minerals** 岩石に含まれていた鉱物　**this inflow of river water adding to ~** = and this inflow of river water adds to ~; inflow of river water 川水の流入．　**adding to the ocean several billion tons of salts** = adding several billion tons of salts to the ocean.　**there is little similarity** 殆んど類似性がない　**chemical composition** 化学組成　**elements** 元素　**proportions** 割合　**bring in ~** ～をもたらす　**four times as much calcium as chloride** = four times as much as (the rivers bring in chloride) 塩化物よりも 4 倍も多いカルシウム　**strongly** まったく

Vocabulary

語頭文字と文字数をヒントに綴りなさい.

01.	貯蔵所	s-(10字)	02.	立方の	c-(5)	03.	1,000兆の	q-(11)	04.	千年間	m-(10)
05.	想定する	a-(6)	06.	海の方へ	s-(7)	07.	僅かに	f-(7)	08.	塩を含んだ	s-(6)
09.	塩分	s-(9)	10.	主要な	p-(7)	11.	マントル	m-(6)	12.	含む	e-(7)
13.	1年間の	a-(6)	14.	流入	i-(6)	15.	10億	b-(7)	16.	奇妙な	c-(7)
17.	類似	s-(10)	18.	様々な	v-(7)	19.	全く	e-(8)	20.	割合	p-(10)
21.	カルシウム	c-(7)	22.	塩化物	c-(8)	23.	全く	s-(8)	24.	逆にする	r-(7)

Q & A

1) What is the greatest storehouse of minerals in the earth?

2) In which direction are the heaviest movements though the earth is constantly shifting her component materials from place to place?

3) Why has it been assumed that the first seas were only faintly saline and that their saltiness has been growing over a long long period?

4) What does the annual flow of about 6,500 cubic miles of water seaward add to the ocean?

5) Is river water similar, in chemical composition, to sea water?

Chapter 15-2 [Grammar Check] 関係詞

31

1. 関係代名詞

1) I have an uncle **who** [**that**] lives abroad. （先行詞「人」，主格）

2) I know a boy **whose** father is a pilot. （先行詞「人」，所有格）

3) He is a man **whom** [**that**] I respect very much. （先行詞「人」，目的格）

4) Look at the picture **which** [**that**] is on the wall. （先行詞「人以外」，主格）

5) The house **whose** roof [the roof of **which**] is red is hers. （先行詞「人以外」，所有格）

6) The question **which** [**that**] I asked him was not easy. （先行詞「人以外」，目的格）

7) **What** he said is true. （先行詞含まれる，主格）

8) He is not **what** he was ten years ago.「10 年前の彼」（先行詞含まれる，主格）

2. 限定用法と継続用法

9) He has two sons **who** want to work for old people. （他にも息子がいる可能性あり）

10) He has two sons**, who** want to work for old people. (= and they)

11) He broke the window**, which** made his father angry. (= and it)

3. おもに that が用いられる場合

12) 先行詞に最上級の形容詞 , the only, the very, the first, all, no などがつくとき

He is **the richest** man **that** I know.

Mr. Yoshino is **the only** person **that** supports me here.

This is **the very** picture **that** I have long wanted to see. （まさにその）

The first student **that** answered the difficult question was my rival.

13) 人と人以外が同時に先行詞になっている場合

Look at **the boy and the dog that** are playing over there.

4. 関係代名詞の省略

14) Tom has several people (**whom**) he has to help. （目的格）(See 1.3) ）

15) This is the bag (**which**) she bought yesterday. （目的格）(See 1.6) ）

16) There is somebody (**that**) wants to see you at the gate. （There be 動詞…の構文内で）

17) This is the best book (**that**) **there is** on the subject. （直後に there be 動詞が続く場合）

18) He is not the man (**that**) he was ten years ago. （be 動詞の補語）

5. 関係副詞

19) I know the day **when** she was born. （時）
cf. He came home at six, **when** we were having dinner. (= and then)

20) That is the house **where** my uncle lives. （場所）
cf. We went to Australia, **where** we stayed for a week. (= and there)

21) Do you know the reason **why** she got angry? （理由）

22) This is **how** [the way] I did it. 「このようにして」（方法）
cf. That is **why** she is crying. 「そのようなわけで …」

Exercises

A. 次の二つの文を関係代名詞を使って一つの文に書き替えなさい．

1. Tanaka is a college student.　He lives in Tokyo.
2. The man was Columbus.　He discovered America.
3. The girl is my sister.　You met her yesterday.
4. I have a friend.　Her mother is a pianist.
5. This is the first letter.　I have received it from my father.

B. 次の文中の（　）内に適当な関係代名詞を入れなさい．

1. They are the students (　　　　) arrived here just now.
2. The mountain (　　　　) top is covered with snow is Mt. Fuji.
3. This is the very book (　　　　) I have wanted to read.
4. A car ran over the old man and his dog (　　　　) were crossing the road.
5. I will lend you this book, (　　　　) you will find interesting.

C. 次の英文を日本文に直しなさい．

1. He gave me all the books that he had.
2. He was the only boy that could answer the question.
3. The building which you see over there is our college.
4. I remained silent, which seemed to irritate him.

D. 次の日本文を（　）内の語句と関係代名詞を使って英文に直しなさい．

1. パリは誰もが訪れたいと思っている都市のひとつです．　(a city, visit)
2. これは私が今まで読んだうちで一番面白い本です．　(have ever)
3. 私は英語の得意な学生を何人か知っています．　(several, good at)
4. 表紙の青い本が私のものです．　(cover)
5. 彼女には娘が三人いるが，３人とも医者です．　(has)

Rearranging

▶▶▶ (　) 内の語に 1 語加えて並べ替え，和文に合う英文にしなさい．

1. 私には米国に住んでいる姉がいます．　(have / lives / the USA / I / sister / in / a).

2. 君の着ている服は汚れている．　(the / on / dirty / clothes / have / are / you).

3. 屋根の見える家は私の叔母のです．(roof / house / see / aunt's / you / is / my / the / can).

4. 人間は火を使用できる唯一の動物です．　(only / can / man / use / is / fire / the / animal).

5. ここは私が子供の頃住んでいた家です．
(this / childhood / is / lived / the / my / I / house / in / in).

6. それが私の言いたかったことです．　(I / that / say / is / to / wanted).

7. 5月は私が生まれた月です．　(born / May / I / month / is / was / the).

Basic Composition

▶▶▶ 文末の（　）内の条件をヒント（動詞は原形で提示）に英訳しなさい．

1. 私はその事件について書いてある本を持っている．　(tells, case を含む 9 語で)

2. 君が会ったその男性は有名な歌手です．　(novel, was を含んで 9 語で)

3. 彼には俊という名の息子がいる．　(関係代名詞を用いて 8 語で)

4. 君の興味を引く本をすべて持っていってよい．　(interest を含んで 9 語で)

5. 彼はいわゆる叩き上げの男だ．　(we, self-made を含んで 8 語で)

6. ここはアリスと初めて会った公園です．　(where を含んで 9 語で)

7. 私が黙っていると彼は怒った．　(remained, which を含んで 7 語で)

8. 私はこのようにして英語を学んだ．　(how を含んで 6 語で)

9. 私は英国に行って，そこで一月滞在した．　(where を含んで 10 語で)

Rewriting ▶▶▶ 次の各組の文がほぼ同じ意味になるように，（　）内に適語を書き入れなさい．

1. The minute I got home, it began to rain.
   = As (　　　　　) as I got home, it began to rain.
2. Did he break the door? = (　　　　　) the door broken by him?
3. We will meet at the airport. = We (　　　　　) to meet at the airport.
4. I am sure they will be in time. = I am sure of their (　　　　　) in time.
5. He is despised by everybody. = He is looked down (　　　　　) by everybody.
6. He drives a bus. It is his work. = (　　　　　) a bus is his work.
7. To the best of my knowledge, he has never been there.
   = As (　　　　　) as I know, he has never been there.
8. He is a pilot. I also want to be a pilot. = He is a pilot, (　　　　　) I also want to be.
9. The church was being built. = The church was (　　　　　) construction.
10. If you don't get up at once, you'll be late. = Get up at once, (　　　　　) you'll be late.

▶▶▶ Road to Science & Tech English (A15) ▶▶▶

Put into English ▶▶▶ 語句を並べ替えて，日本文に合う英文にしなさい．

1. 水は熱すると 100 度になるまで温度上昇を続けるが，100 度に達すると一定温度を保つ．しかし，数分間沸騰すると，お湯がいく分減ることがわかろう．

   When (the water / heated, / 100℃ / continues / rising to / and / is maintained / that temperature). (will / , however, / it / be noted / boiling water / that / is reduced / the volume of / slightly after boiling / for several / continues) minutes.

   ....

   ....

2. 寒いと水道管は凍ります．特に屋外に出ている水道管がその被害を受けやすいといえます．水は凍ると膨張するので，水道管が破裂することになります．凍るのを少しでも防ぐのにボロを巻く方法があります．

   In (water / cold weather, / in water pipes, / may freeze / are exposed to / especially if / the weather outdoors / they). Since (expands when / water / it freezes, / will burst / the pipe / it). One (methods to prevent / is to cover / of the effective / the pipes / with / freezing) rags.

   ....

   ....

   ....

人称代名詞の一覧表 **The List of Personal Pronouns（Chapter 4）**

	人称	主 格〜 は(が)	所有格〜 の	目的格 〜に(を)	所有代名詞 〜のもの	再帰代名詞 〜自身
単数	1	I	my	me	mine	myself
	2	you	your	you	yours	yourself
	3	he	his	him	his	himself
		she	her	her	hers	herself
		it	its	it	—	itself
複数	1	we	our	us	ours	ourselves
	2	you	your	you	yours	yourselves
	3	they	their	them	theirs	themselves

関係代名詞 **Relative Pronouns（Chapter 15）**

先行詞／格	主格	所有格	目的格
人	who	whose	whom
人以外	which	whose	which
何でもよい	that	—	that
なし	what	—	what

English Proverbs（英語のことわざ）

1. A bird in the hand is worth two in the bush.　明日の百より今日の五十.
2. Do in Rome as the Romans do.　郷に入っては郷に従え.
3. Easier said than done.　言うは易く行うは難し.
4. Care killed a cat.　心配が猫を殺した.（心配は身の毒.）
5. First come, first served.　先んずれば人を制す.
6. Great hopes make great men.　大望は偉人を作る.
7. A friend in need is a friend indeed.　まさかの時の友こそ真の友.
8. Heaven helps those who help themselves.　天は自ら助くる者を助く.
9. Honesty is the best policy.　正直は最良の策である.
10. It is no use crying over spilt milk.　覆水盆にかえらず.
11. Little by little one goes far.　千里の道も一歩より.
12. Make haste slowly.　急がばまわれ.
13. Many men, many minds.　十人十色.
14. Never put off till tomorrow what may be done today.　今日できる事を明日に延すな.
15. Out of sight , out of mind.　去る者は日々に疎し.
16. Practice makes perfect.　習うよりは慣れよ.
17. Rome was not built in a day.　ローマは一日にして成らず.
18. Second thoughts are best.　再考したことが最上である.
19. Slow and steady wins the race.　ゆっくりと着実にやれば競争に勝つ.
20. There is no royal road to learning.　学問に王道なし.
21. A little neglect may breed a great mischief.　小なる怠慢は大なる災いの元となる.
22. First deserve and then desire.　まず実力を養え，それから希望せよ.
23. He that burns most shines most.　最もよく燃えるものは最も輝く.（栄誉は努力次第.）
24. Tomorrow is another day.　明日は明日の風が吹く.
25. The shortest answer is doing.　最も短い返答は行うことである.
26. There is a pleasure that is born of pain.　苦痛から生まれる快楽がある.（苦は楽の種.）
27. He goes far that never turns.　曲がらずに行くものは遠くへ行く.
28. Do to others as you would be done by.　己の欲するところを人に施せ.
29. Cut your coat according to your cloth.　布地に応じて服を裁断せよ.（分相応に暮せ.）
30. Make hay while the sun shines.　陽の照るうちに干し草を作れ.（好機逃がすべからず.）
31. Two heads are better than one.　3人寄れば文殊の知恵.
32. The early bird catches the worm.　早起き鳥が虫を捕まえる.（早起きは三文の得.）
33. The darkest hour is that before the dawn.　一番暗いのは夜明け前.（最悪の状態は好転の兆し.）

Let's Enjoy Science & Tech English [B-913]
教養課程の科学技術英語

1 刷 2021年 2月 5日
2 刷 2023年 3月13日

著 者 佐藤 哲三 Tetsuzo SATO
棈松 伸二 Shinji ABEMATSU
鞍掛 哲治 Tetsuharu KURAKAKE
篠田 義明 Yoshiaki SHINODA

発行者 南雲 一範 Kazunori Nagumo
発行所 株式会社 南雲堂
〒162-0801 東京都新宿区山吹町361
NAN'UN-DO Co., Ltd.
361 Yamabuki-cho, Shinjuku-ku, Tokyo 162-0801, Japan
振替口座 : 00160-0-46863
TEL: 03-3268-2311（代表）／FAX: 03-3269-2486
編集者 加藤 敦

製 版 加藤 敦

装 丁 Nスタジオ

検 印 省 略

コード ISBN978-4-523-17913-9 C0082

Printed in Japan

E-mail nanundo@post.email.ne.jp
URL https://www.nanun-do.co.jp/